Flaminio Gualdoni

AF544876

IMPRESSIONISM

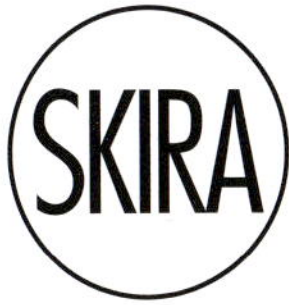

front cover
Claude Monet
Impression, soleil levant
(*Impression, Sunrise*) (detail),
1872
Oil on canvas, 48 x 63 cm
Musée Marmottan Monet, Paris

Skira editore
SkiraMiniARTbooks

Editor
Eileen Romano

Design
Marcello Francone

Editorial Coordination
Giovanna Rocchi

Editing
Maria Conconi

Layout
Anna Cattaneo

Iconographical Research
Marta Tosi

Translation
Dick Nowell for Language
Consulting Congressi, Milan

First published in Italy in 2008
by Skira Editore S.p.A.
Palazzo Casati Stampa
via Torino 61
20123 Milano
Italy

www.skira.net

No part of this book may be
reproduced or utilized in any form
or by any means, electronic
or mechanical, including
photocopying, recording, or any
information storage and retrieval
system, without permission
in writing from the publisher.

© 2008 by Skira editore
All rights reserved under
international copyright
conventions.

Printed and bound in Italy.
First edition

ISBN 978-88-6130-738-4

Distributed in the US and Canada
through Rizzoli International
Publications by Random House,
300 Park Avenue South,
New York, NY 10010.
Distributed elsewhere in the world
by Thames and Hudson Ltd.,
181a High Holborn, London
WC1V 7QX, United Kingdom.

facing title page
Frédéric Bazille
The artist's studio
(detail), 1870
Oil on canvas, 98.5 x 128.5 cm
Musée d'Orsay, Paris

© Photo RMN – © Jean-Gilles
Berizzi, Thierry Le Mage,
Hervé Lewandowski, René-Gabriel
Ojéda – Réunion des Musées
Nationaux / distr. Alinari
© Foto Archivio Scala, Firenze,
2008
Archivio Skira

Works owned by the
Soprintendenza are published
by permission of the Ministero
per i Beni e le Attività Culturali

The publisher is at the disposal
of the entitled parties as regards
all unidentified iconographic
and literary sources.

Contents

Impressionism

On 25 April 1874 the satirical Parisian daily "Le Charivari" published an account by the artist and man of letters Louis Leroy of his visit to the exhibition by the "Société Anonyme coopérative d'artistes-peintres, sculpteurs, graveurs et lithographes" which had opened ten days earlier in the former studio of the photographer Nadar at 35 Boulevard des Capucines. 165 works were on show, by thirty artists – from Pierre-Auguste Renoir to Eugène Boudin, from Edgar Degas to Berthe Morisot – who declared their intention of no longer following the art system's official rules, firstly because they painted freely and not by academic prescription, and secondly because they rejected the rigmarole of acceptance at the Salons, the official exhibitions to which entry was through the assessment of a jury – whose competence and authority they did not recognise.

Leroy tells of being accompanied by Joseph Vincent, a landscape artist "honoured by more than one government", and of how both were (ironically) stunned by the new painting. Standing before Camille Pissarro's cabbage field in *Une matinée du mois de juin* their comment is: "Oh, poor things; how they've been caricatured. I swear I'll never eat another as long as I live." And in front of a Monet: "What does this canvas represent? Let's see the list: *Impression, soleil levant*. Impression, I thought as much. I was impressed, and I thought to myself, yes, there's bound to be an impression in there somewhere... But frankly, designs for wallpaper are more finished than this seascape!"

And so the term "Impressionism" was born, the first in a long line of derogatory labels which the avant-gardes of the late 19th and early 20th centuries, from "Fauves" to "Cubists", would proudly and pugnaciously adopt as official titles.

The course of the Impressionist movement, however, matured long

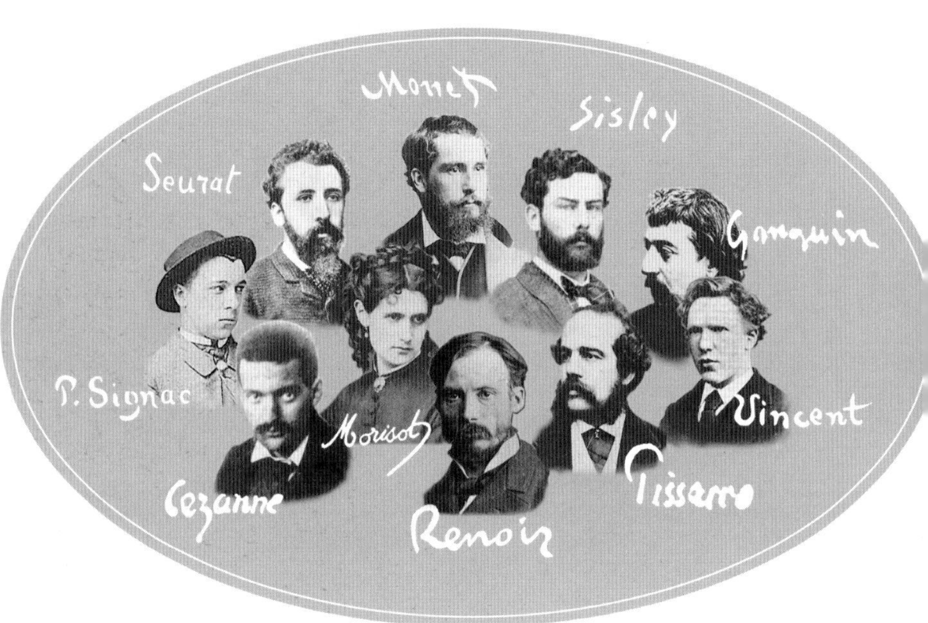
Monet
Sisley
Seurat
Gauguin
P. Signac
Vincent
Morisot
Cezanne
Pissarro
Renoir

before 1874 and that fateful exhibition at Nadar's. Already around the 1850's painters like Gustave Courbet or the Barbizon School led by Camille Corot had been accused of moving away from the institutional path of properly finished, finely crafted painting on the model of the Old Masters, wholly worked out in the studio. Corot painted in the open air, in the presence of his subject; he paid attention to his feelings, to the affective relationship with what he was seeing: "I interpret with my heart as much as with my eye", he used to say. Courbet, for his part, was a revolutionary in politics as well, and preferred "low" subjects from popular life, depicting them with a rough and ready realism, deliberately choosing unfinished effects and stylistic short-cuts that could be harsh, even unsightly. Excluded from the Universal Exhibition of 1855, he challenged the cultural authorities by presenting forty canvases in the Pavillon du Réalisme in avenue Montaigne, off the official circuit.

Impressionists and their signatures

The spiritual father of the movement, however, was Édouard Manet: Morisot sat for him, became his sister-in-law in 1874, and painted longer than he did. His *Le Déjeuner sur l'Herbe* was rejected at the official Salon in 1863 (with some 4000 other entries): but so loud were the protests that Napoleon III was obliged to set up a Salon des Refusés in which works rejected by the official one might be shown – thus admitting the relative nature of the judging (by a panel of members of the Académie des Beaux-Arts and previous Salon exhibitors), and the existence of artistic currents opposed to those that had the blessing of the cultural authorities. Manet himself never took part in any of the shows of the Impressionist group, preferring the contest of the Salons ("at the Salon even my most savage detractors have to march past me", he argued); nevertheless, he became their accepted authority, and to his younger admirers – not only the painters Monet, Renoir, Degas, Pissarro, Alfred Sisley and Frédéric Bazille, but also the writer Émile Zola and the photographer Nadar – he would time and again declare, among the tables of the Café Guerbois in grand-rue des Batignolles (today avenue de Clichy), "I paint what I see, not what others like to see". And what he painted came from the notebooks in which he sketched his impressions of the teeming life of Paris. His friend Antonin Proust later wrote of him: "Paris has never known an idler who idled more profitably [than Manet]. He woul draw a trifle, a profile, a hat, in a word a fugitive impression."

Paul Cézanne
The House of the Hanged Man (detail), 1872-73
Oil on canvas, 55 × 66 cm
Musée d'Orsay, Paris

With Manet as intellectual godfather, the "Groupe des Batignolles", the kernel that gave rise to Impressionism, began to form around 1869 at the Café Guerbois; it was meetings there that drafted the Articles of Association of the "Société Anonyme", whose birth was announced by Monet on 17 January 1874 in the *Chronique des Arts*. It is perhas worth noting that when, in 1920, Marcel Duchamp, Man Ray and Katherine Dreier founded their New York group to promote the art of the avant-garde, they called it "Société Anonyme, Inc.", in homage to Monet and his companions.

What these artists had in common, though their variety embraced anyone drawn to a direct and affective naturalism, was that they valued the unfiltered rendering of visual feelings above descriptive precision, fine composition, or studied and elaborate painting; and that they gave as much importance to the living presence of what they portrayed – life as it is, including the ordinary contingencies of reality; nature, living and never static, as it is presented to the eye in

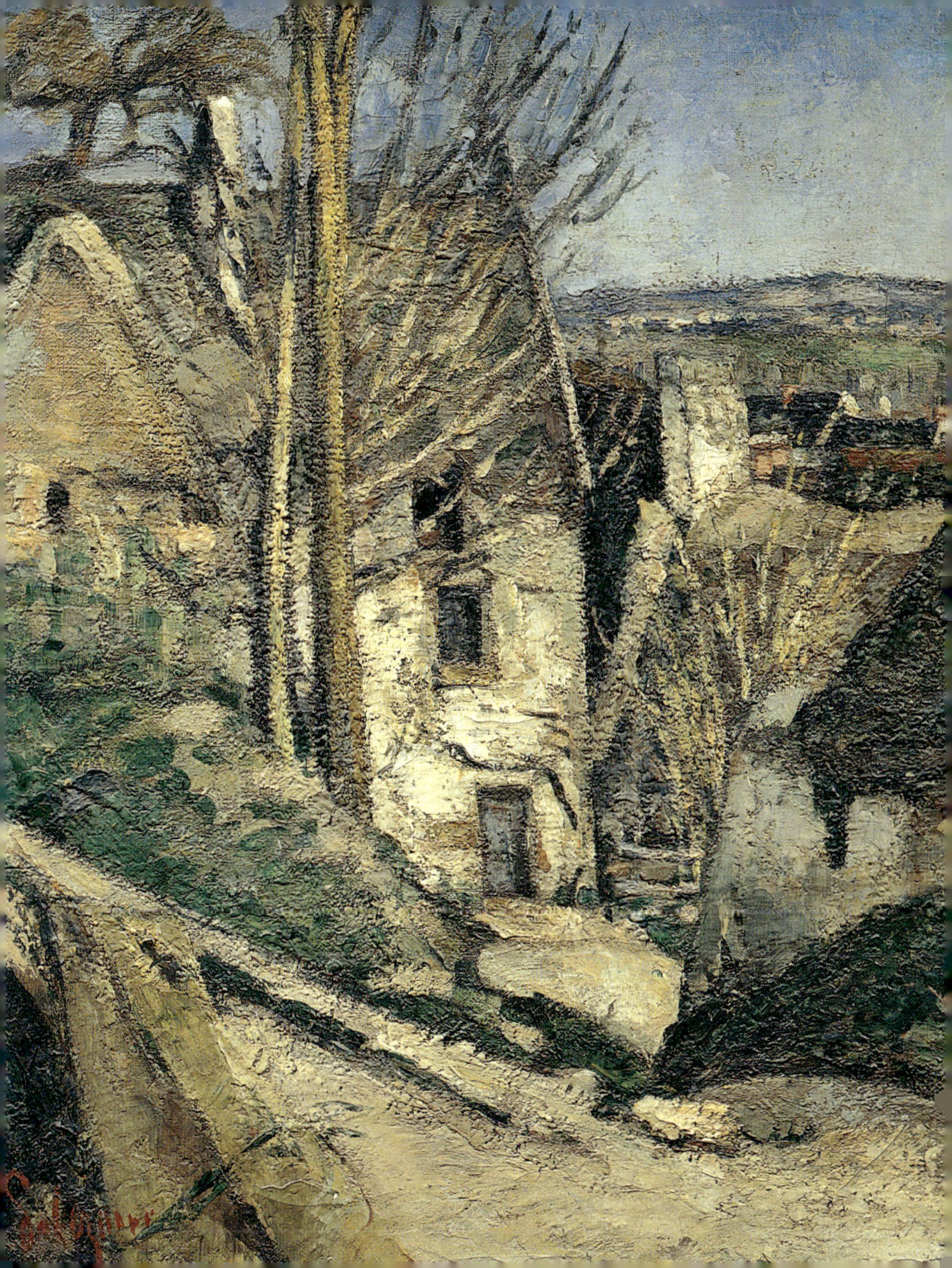

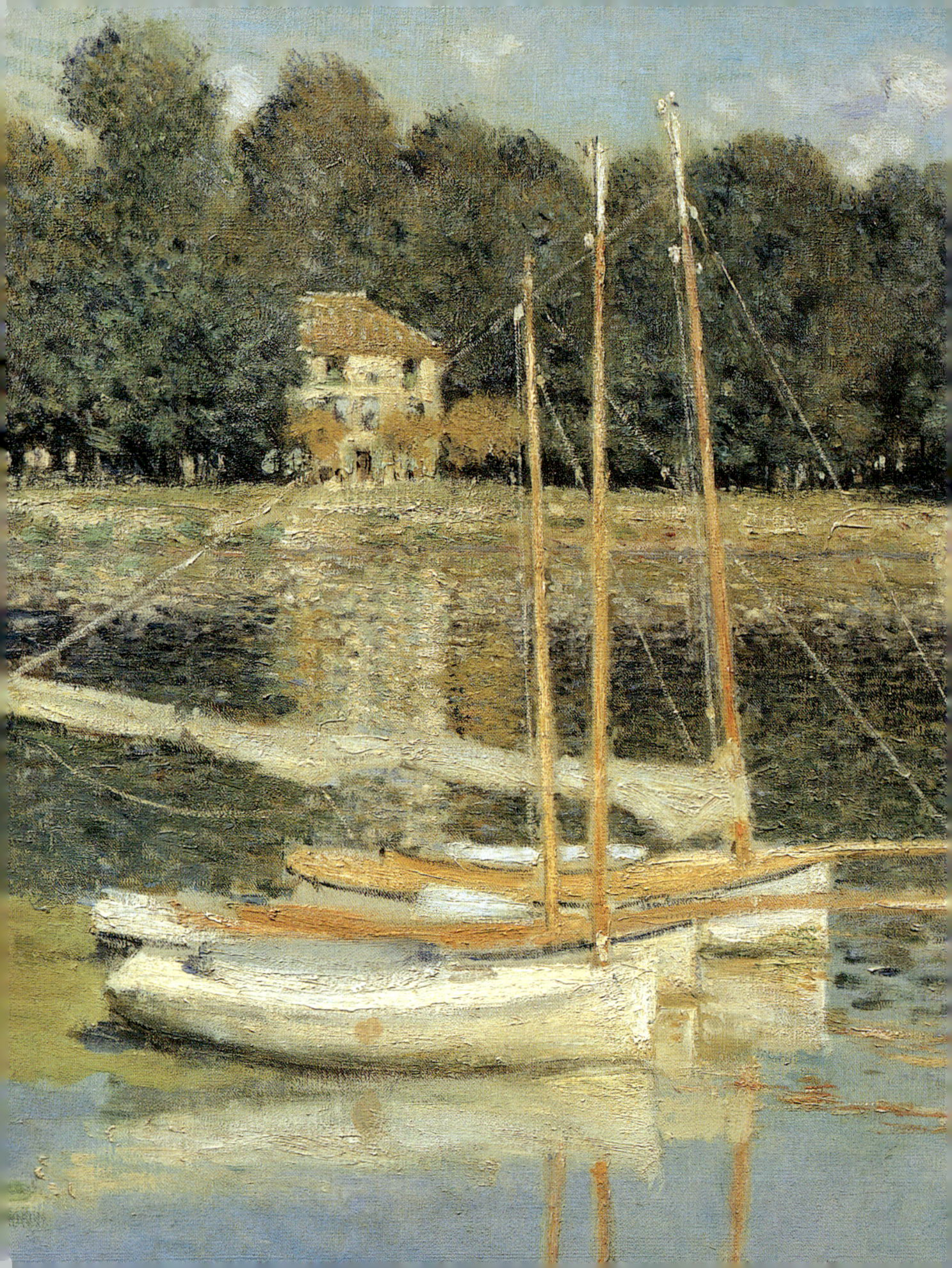

changes of light and weather – as to the analysis of what the eye perceives, which is considered much more important than the intellect's mental selections and reorganizations.

Some rapidly enjoyed a certain acclaim and, though sales were modest to start with, came to be regarded as authorities at least within the artistic world: Monet, Pissarro, Sisley, Degas, Renoir, all identified, together with Manet, as the coming artists by the inspired and open-minded dealer Paul Durand-Ruel. Others, such as the Italian Giuseppe De Nittis and Leon-Paul Robert, Louis Debras, Louis Latouche, Ludovic Napoléon Lepic, Alfred Meyer, Émilien Mulot Durivage, Adolphe-Félix Cals, or Henri Rouart, were to have less well-defined careers and less recognizable styles.

Claude Monet
The bridge at Argenteuil
(detail), 1874
Oil on canvas, 60.5 × 80 cm
Musée d'Orsay, Paris

The part played by Durand-Ruel while Impressionism was at this stage, and subsequently in the days of its international success, was a decisive one. He was a dealer in the modern sense; indeed he was the first to apply some rules which later became usual in the art world – individual exhibitions, entry free of charge to shows in his gallery, exclusive dealerships, use of the press as an instrument of promotion, a determined readiness to take risks on new art and an appreciation of the good financial rewards that were possible, and finally the idea of setting up an international network of galleries.

The 1874 exhibition at the Nadar studio brought in only 3500 francs in sales (Cézanne's *The house of the Hanged Man*, for instance, was bought for 200 francs by a collector, Count Doria); but even two years earlier, when Durand-Ruel presented some of these artists in his London gallery, he spent 12,000 francs on works by Monet; and in 1885, at a time when a top civil servant earned 20,000 francs a year, this resolutely sanguine dealer was a million francs in debt.

His was an open-minded stance, thoroughly vindicated in the end. At the time of the Impressionists' second show, which he organized in 1876, his gallery was described quite simply as "a madhouse"; but the one he organized ten years later in New York triggered the American collectors' passion for the movement, and he began to get legendary prices for these works. It has been calculated that by the time he died in 1922 Durand-Ruel had bought some 12,000 paintings, including approximately 1000 Monets, 1500 Renoirs and 800 Pissarros.

One of the factors in Impressionism's success was precisely that air of scandal, visual provocation, and broken traditions stirred up by this kind of painting. It was not until 1878, and a show put on by Durand-Ruel himself, that the Barbizon School itself was accepted by the official culture as an artistic vein worthy of some respect; but the world of art and taste was much less able to understand the more radical Impressionist painting, which broke too many of the rules generally regarded as unshakeable and sacrosanct: this young generation of artists was condemned for its unfinished feel, the fluidity of the brushstrokes, the apparent facility and formal banality of the compositions, and the clarity of hues which, by comparison with academic painting and its Creed based on shadows and earth colours, seemed off-scale.

Leroy's words, in his fateful review of 1874, are symptomatic: he says of Joseph Vincent at this exhibition that "he thought he would see the kind of paintings one sees anywhere, good and bad, rather bad than good, but not hostile to good artistic manners, respect for form, obedience to the masters. Ah, form! Alas, the masters! They are no longer needed, my poor friend! All that has changed!"

"Paris has never known an idler who idled more profitably [than Manet]. He woul draw a trifle, a profile, a hat, in a word a fugitive impression."

Antonin Proust

Pierre-Auguste Renoir
Monet painting in his garden at Argenteuil, 1873
Oil on canvas, 46 × 60 cm
Wadsworth Athenaeum Museum, Hartford

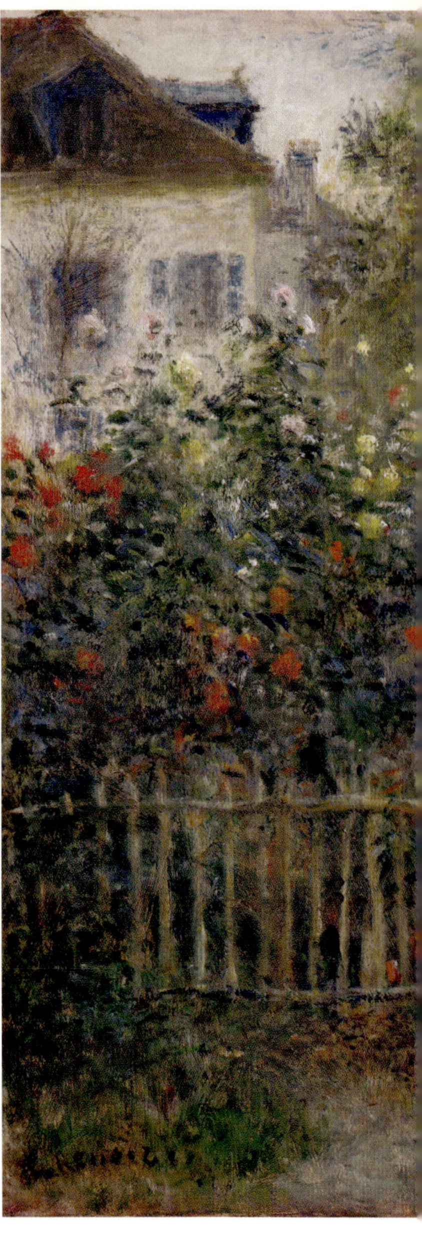

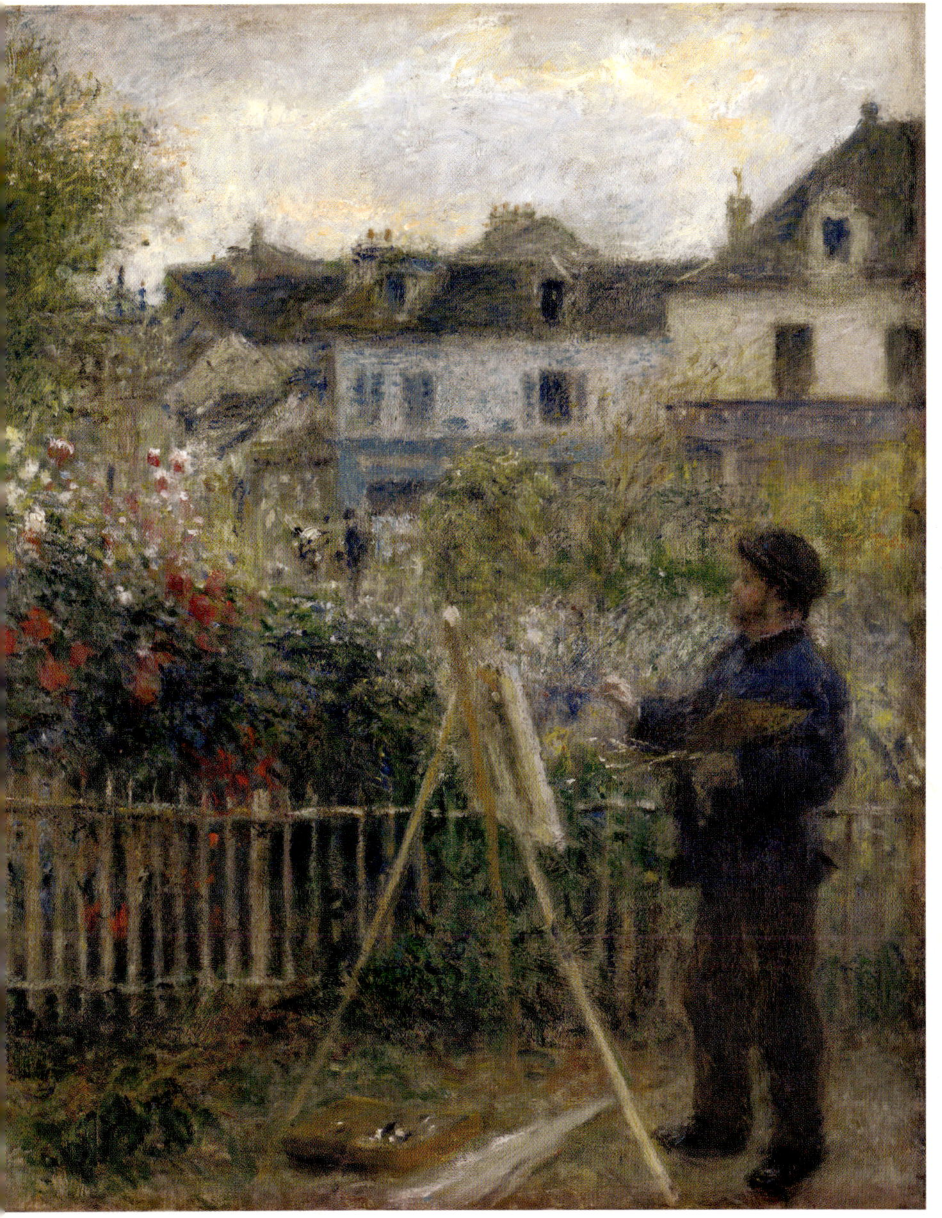

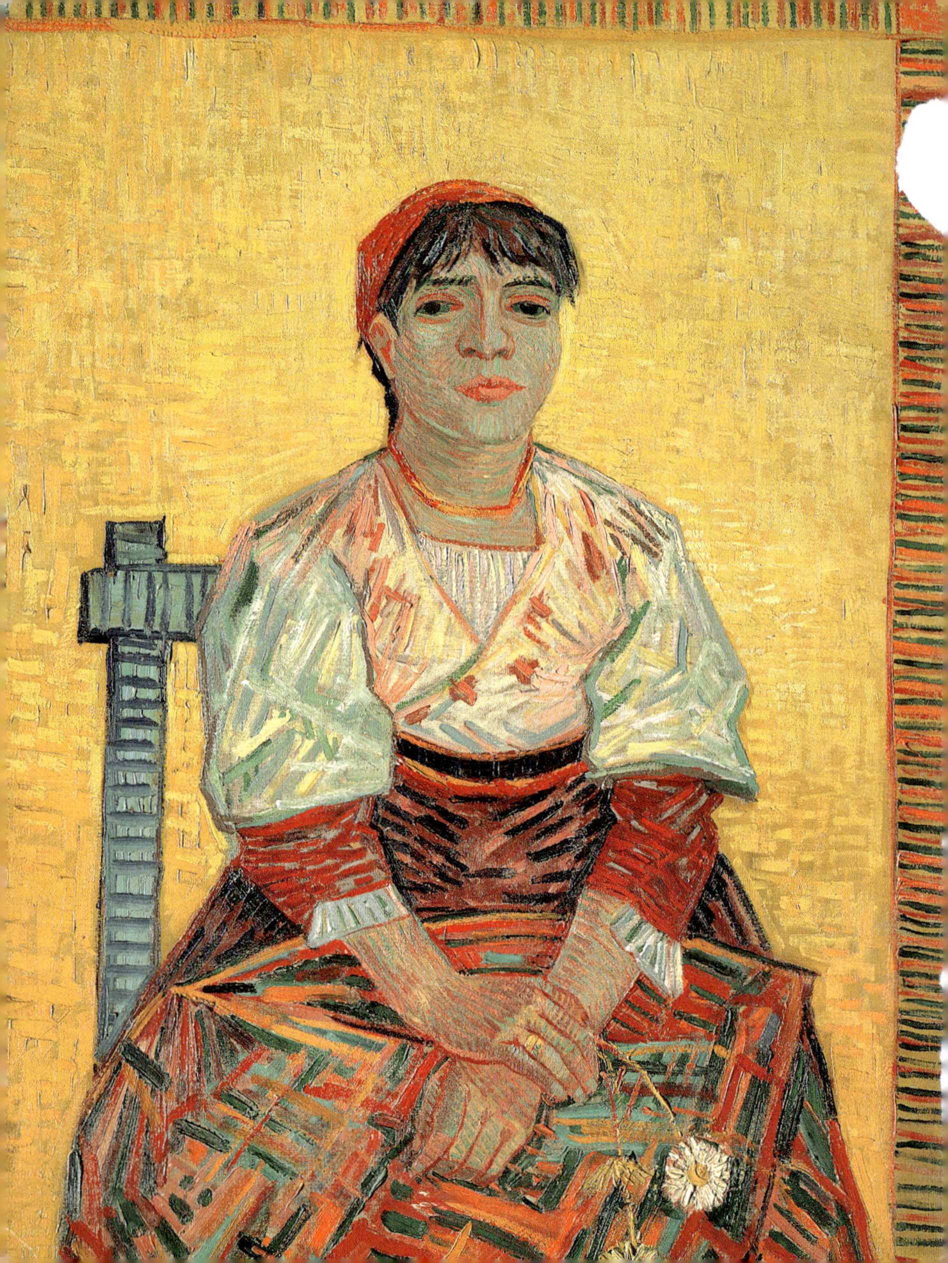

direct visual sensation, to the study of the way forms interact with light, in a relationship to reality not mediated by intellectual preconceptions.

The touchstone that revealed the true devotee (and the height of scandal for the detractors) was Monet. Enlightened by J.M.W. Turner's experimental daring, Monet had since the early 1870s abandoned geometrical perspective and the tidy definition of planes, and sought to capture the fluidity of the atmosphere, the way one colour would gradually merge into another until they became a single vision in which indeterminate continuity was more important than spatial architecture, and colour's effect – including its emotional effect – more important than its accuracy.

Impressionism's critical fellow-traveller Cézanne (he only irregularly jointed in the shows) said "Monet's only an eye – yet what an eye!": a perfect summary of his friend's extraordinary ability to look and see in such a way as to restore the sense of physical and emotional fullness that people feel in front of the light-filled, moving spectacle of nature or the city. Morisot, again, speaking of his ability to render the luminosity of the season and the time of day so abundantly: "Looking at a Monet painting, I always know which way to tilt my umbrella"; and finally Zola, when (in an article in *Le Voltaire* of June 1880) he summed up the idea of Impressionism as "meticulous study of the causes and effects of light, which influences line as well as colour", he was surely thinking in the first place of Monet.

Much in the same way as Monet, with his luminosity of colour and iridescent motion between light and shade rendered as hues, comes a painter like Renoir, who (in such emblematic compositions of the Impressionist era as *Bal au Moulin de la Galette*, 1876, bought immediately by Gustave Caillebotte who was a patron as well as a member of the group) combined an unbridled tonality – in the relations between light and shade, in the fine interweaving of brushstrokes – with a taste *à la Zola* for the life of ordinary Parisians and for the Bohemian life of Montmartre.

Next to Monet and Renoir come the more cautious Alfred Sisley and Berthe Morisot: the luministic, more compositionally supple wing of Impressionism; for the movement did not, atypically, have a single intellectual leader to construct an unequivocal model for its style; Zola indeed regretted this, thinking it a limitation.

Different is the story of Degas, who moved from classical and realistic arrangements to the open-minded use of viewpoints and the physical incidence of light, considerably helped by his thorough understanding of photographic technique. Never allowing the solidity of the drawing to be compromised by a tremulous medium, in his maturity he typically used pastel, a technique obsolete since the 18th century, opening a path for Toulouse-Lautrec.

Edgar Degas
The Ballet Class
(detail), 1871-74
Oil on canvas, 85 × 75 cm
Musée d'Orsay, Paris

Cézanne, the movement's oddest and most prickly representative and always kept somewhat apart from it by nagging intellectual doubts until before long he left it entirely, was closest in approach to Pissarro. What linked him to the older artist – Corot's fellow-Barbizonian and veteran of the 1863 Salon des Refusés – was an idea of naturalness which selects the perception and the affective climate of a vision but in order to render it in a solid painting, which renews but does not dissolve the architectural feel of the composition: according to Cézanne, Pissarro was "the painter who got closest to nature", meaning to its vital secret and its hidden patterns.

The Impressionist exhibition of 1877 was the one in which the artists

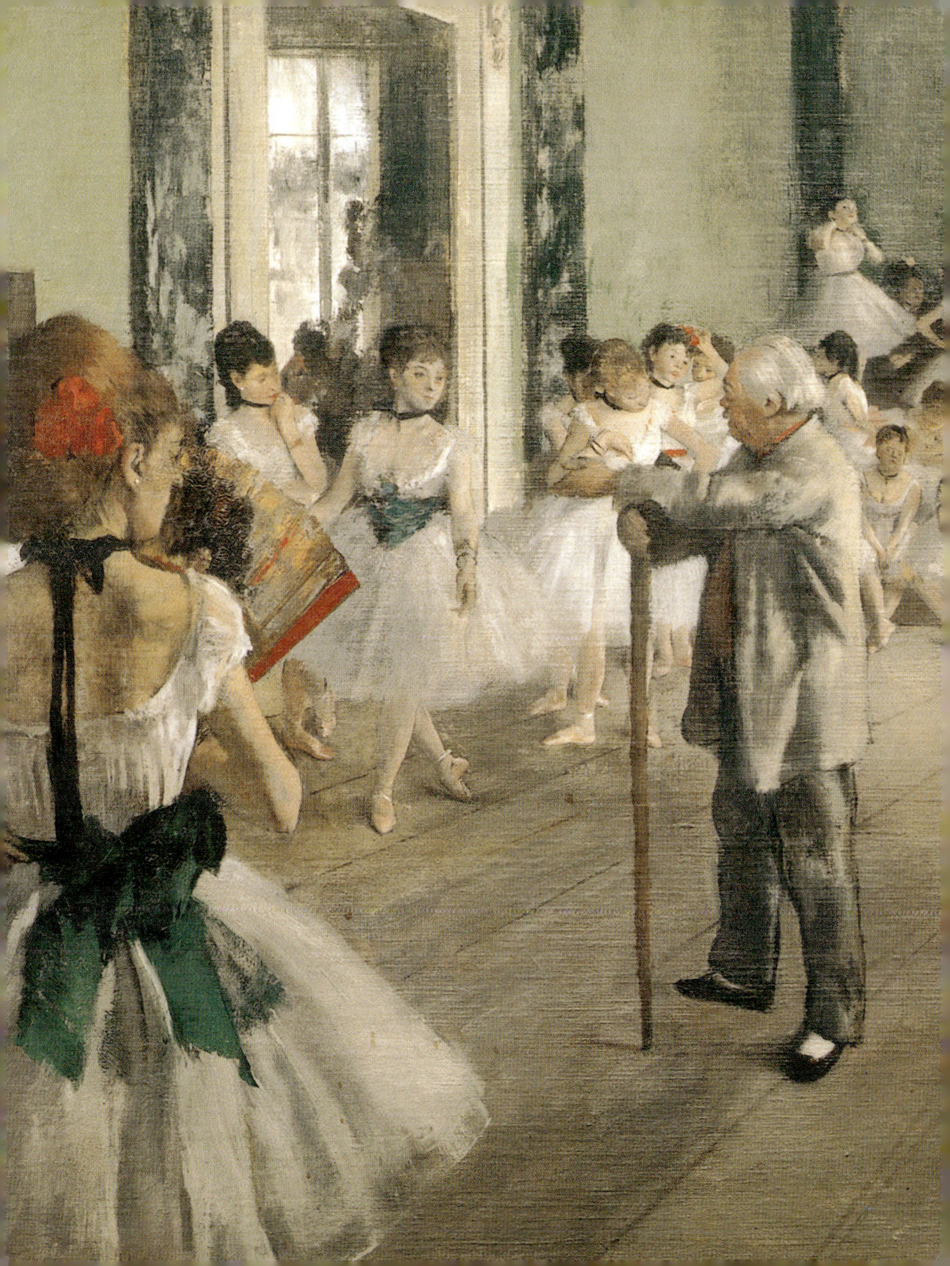

really tried to present themselves as a compact group, whatever the (considerable) differences in their works and ideas. Renoir, Monet, Degas, Cézanne, Pissarro, Sisley, Caillebotte, Morisot, Guillaumin aimed at delineating a unified intellectual attitude as well, a draft of a theory that could serve as the group's watchword.

Shortly afterwards, however, the divergences began to overshadow the affinities. In addition to the different paths each of the artists saw ahead in their own evolution, there were another sources of division: the line to be taken towards the official art world, the individual relationship of each to his or her own ideas of a career, of success.

There were lively discussions at the Nouvelle Athènes in place Pigalle, the *café* they chose as their new meeting place, between those who saw the Salon as the inevitable avenue for their own ambition (Monet, Renoir and Sisley) and the implacable opponents of the official exhibition, from Pissarro to Degas and from Caillebotte to Guillaumin.

The breach was not to be repaired, and its effects also echoed through the later Impressionist shows, where for different reasons Cézanne, Renoir, Sisley and Guillaumin did not exhibit. However, new adherents made up the numbers, starting with the American Mary Cassatt, close friend of Degas, and the Italian Federico Zandomeneghi.

The latter reached Paris in 1874 after ten years in the Tuscan circle of painters known as the "Macchiaioli": Telemaco Signorini, Giuseppe Abbati, Adriano Cecioni, Giovanni Fattori, Silvestro Lega, Cristiano Banti, Odoardo Borrani, Raffaello Sernesi, Vincenzo Cabianca, and Vito d'Ancona, who gathered around the Caffé Michelangelo in Florence and the Castiglioncello seaside villa of Diego Martelli, a writer and patron who in 1867 founded the *Gazzettino delle arti del disegno* and in 1873 the *Giornale artistico*, and who joined Zandomeneghi in Paris in 1878-79.

Oddly enough, it was the older artist Pissarro who was most enthusiastic about the young painters' new theories, and who lent his authority to a grouping that was at least intended to be less litigious and more open to novelty than the now historic "Batignolles Group".

This grouping aimed to return to the anti-institutional spirit of the Salon des Refusés, and took the view that only a public exhibition of everything being produced in the *ateliers* of the new art, without any form of selection, could properly convey the creative fervour of the time, the myriad routes of experimentation with and thinking about paint.

Vincent van Gogh
Cafe Terrace at Night, Place du Forum, Arles, 1888
Oil on canvas, 81 × 65.5 cm
Kröller-Müller Museum, Otterlo

So the Salon des Indépendants came into being in 1884, blessed by Pissarro's authority, and contributed to by Cézanne and Gauguin as well as new artists like Henri de Toulouse-Lautrec, Albert Dubois-Pillet, Odilon Redon, Henri-Edmond Cross, Charles Angrand, Georges Seurat and Paul Signac. Their Articles of Association ran: "The Company of Independent Artists, based on the abolition of the Admissions Panel, has as its object the enabling of artists to present their works to the public's consideration with complete freedom."

By now the original Impressionist group was a memory. Pissarro, who was increasingly finding a new vocation in encouraging the young, insisted that his protégés Signac and Seurat be admitted to the Impressionist exhibition of 1886, which was in fact the last: there Seurat showed his *A Sunday on La Grande Jatte*, at once the manifesto and culmination of *pointillisme*. Pissarro cared little if that mean Monet, Renoir and Sisley refused to exhibit this time. He realized that it had been years since the Impressionists had existed as a group, and that the work of those masters – which he still respected and valued – no longer represented the mainstream of the art of the future.

Monet moved to Giverny in 1883; Pissarro himself to Eragny; Cézanne left Paris for good, moving to Aix-in-Provence. Even a master like Renoir declared: "Around 1883 there was a kind of break in my work; I had gone to the limits of Impressionism and I had reached the conclusion that I could neither paint nor draw. In a word, I was at a dead end." Extricating himself was a brilliant triumph, but took him a long way from what he had been painting before.

Pierre-Auguste Renoir
Portrait of Ambroise Vollard, 1908
Oil on canvas, 81 × 64 cm
Courtauld Institute Galleries, London

1886 saw the last exhibition by the Impressionist group but also, as we have seen, the beginnings of their international success, thanks to Durand-Ruel's New York exhibition which brought together all the historic masters: Monet, Pissarro, Renoir, Degas, Sisley, Morisot, Seurat, Signac and Guillaumin.

It was Guillaumin who made another "discovery" that marked 1886. Auguste Portier, an art dealer who already worked with Durand-Ruel, introduced him to a young Dutchman recently arrived in Paris, whom he was showing around the Ville Lumière for the first time: his name was Vincent van Gogh. The new generation was at hand, a generation which took as its Creed the motto of the old Cézanne: "Painting means thinking with a brush".

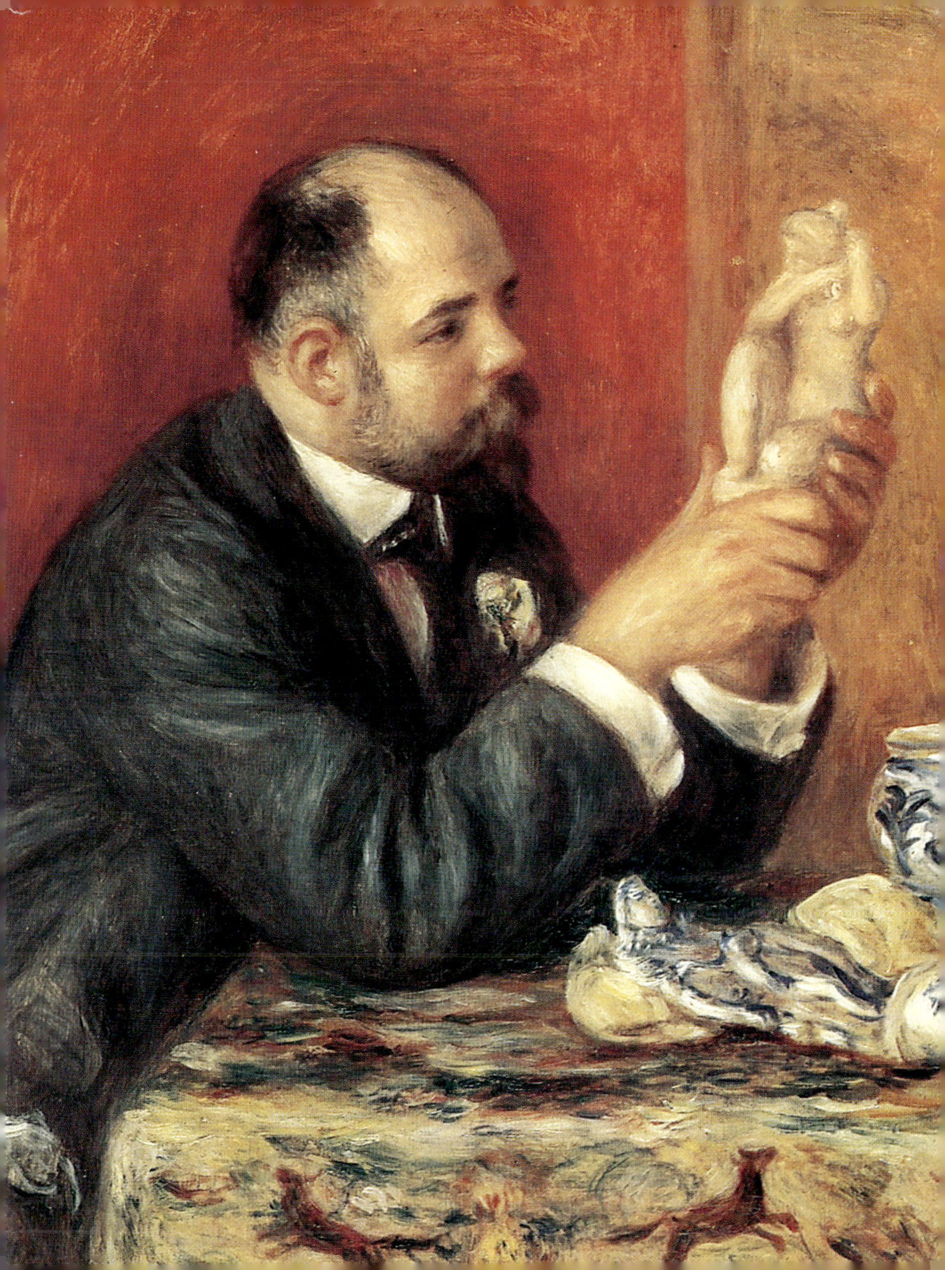

Salon • Salon des Refusés •
En plein air • Café Guerboi
hues • Visual emotions • Art
of Academies • Photography

dividual exhibitions • Colour •
Atmospheric effects • Pure
alers • Impression • Rejection
Light • Modern life •

Works

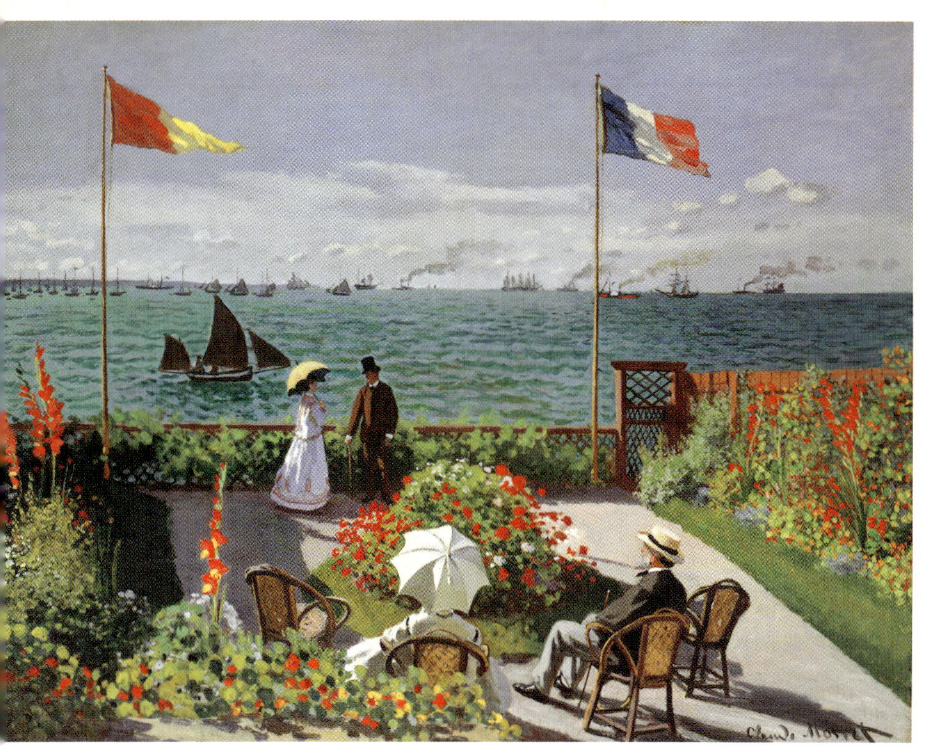

1. Claude Monet
Garden at Sainte-Adresse, 1867

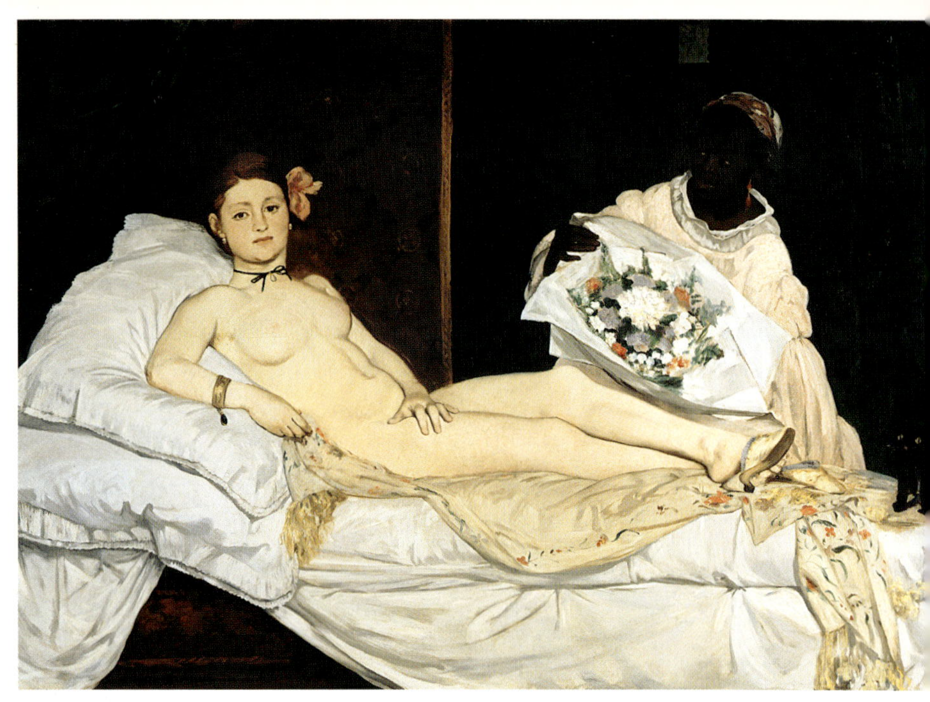

2. Édouard Manet
Olympia, 1863

3. Édouard Manet
Le Déjeuner sur l'Herbe
(The Luncheon on the Grass),
1863

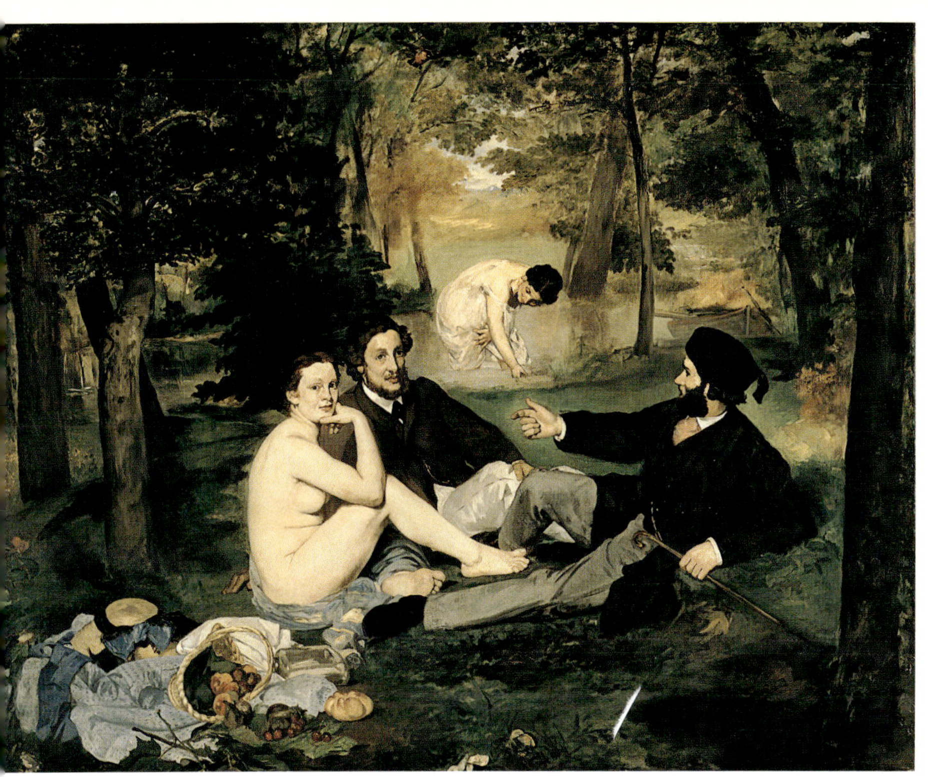

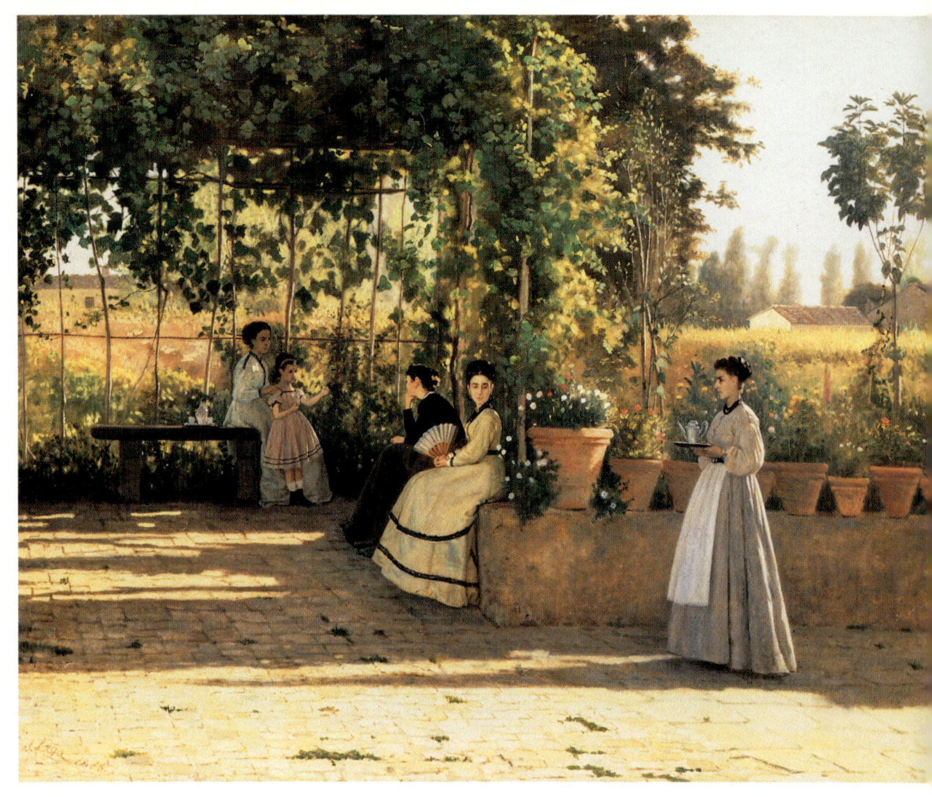

4. Silvestro Lega
After Dinner
(The Pergola), 1868

5. Claude Monet
Women in the Garden, 1867

Following pages
6. Pierre-Auguste Renoir
The Pergola, 1876

7. Pierre-Auguste Renoir
The Swing, 1876

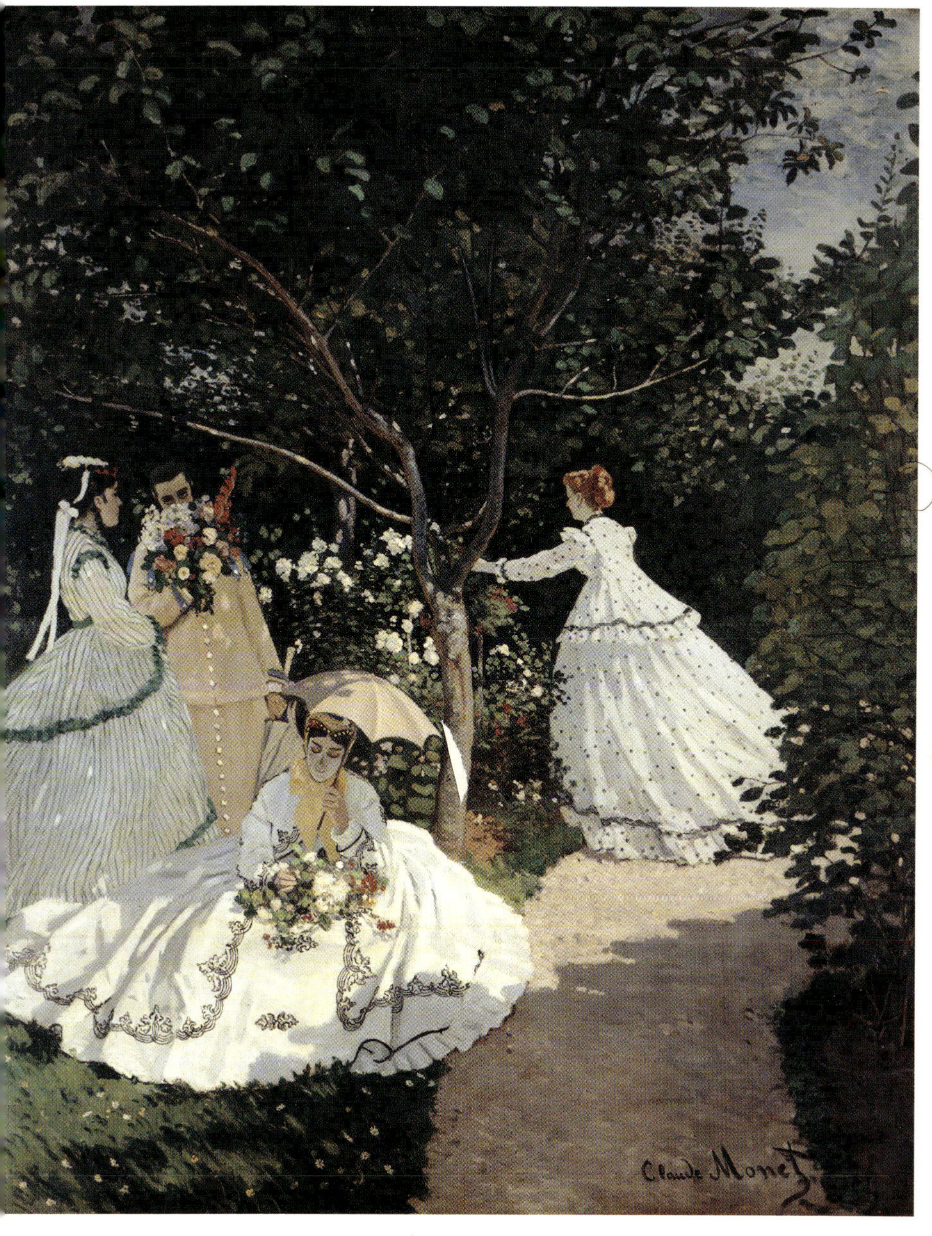
Claude Monet

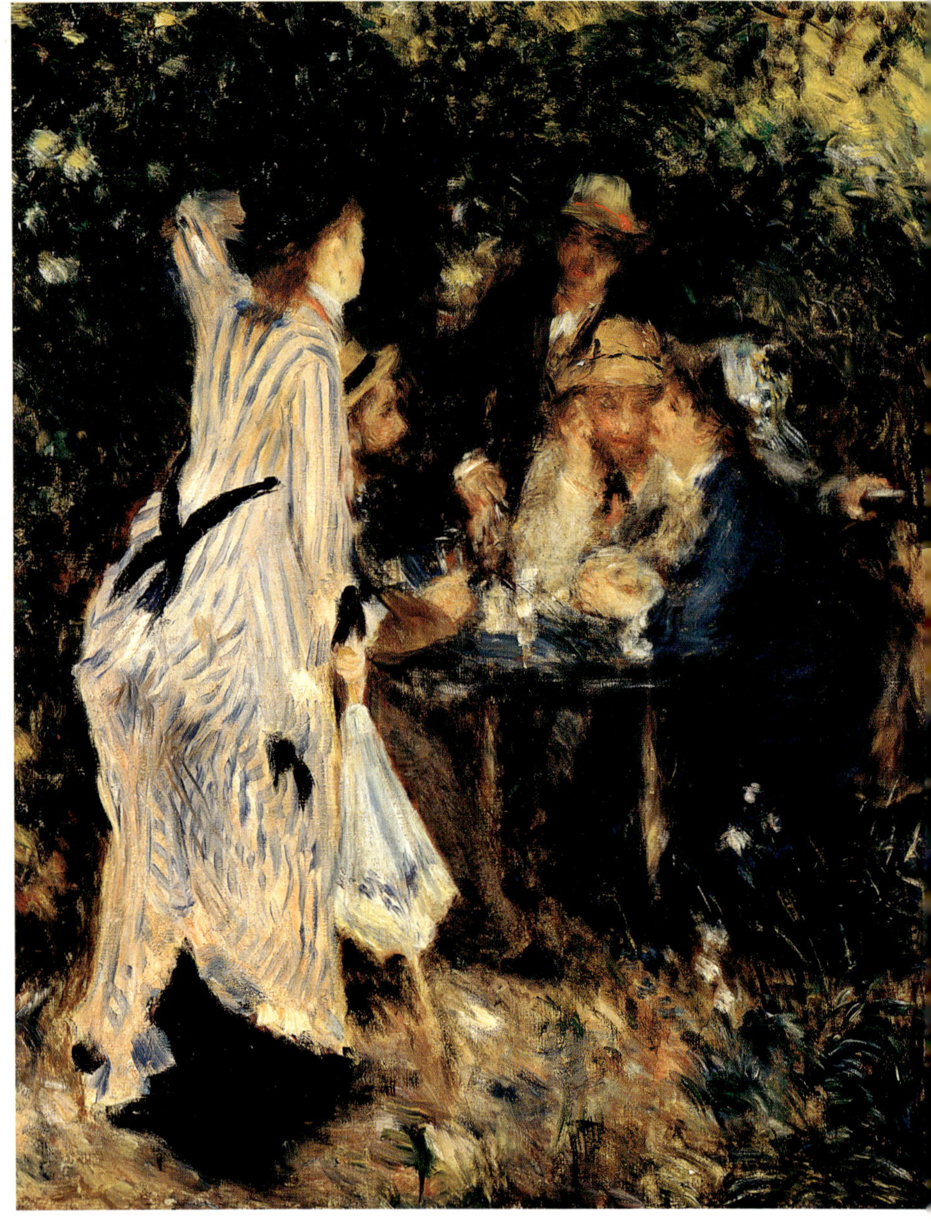

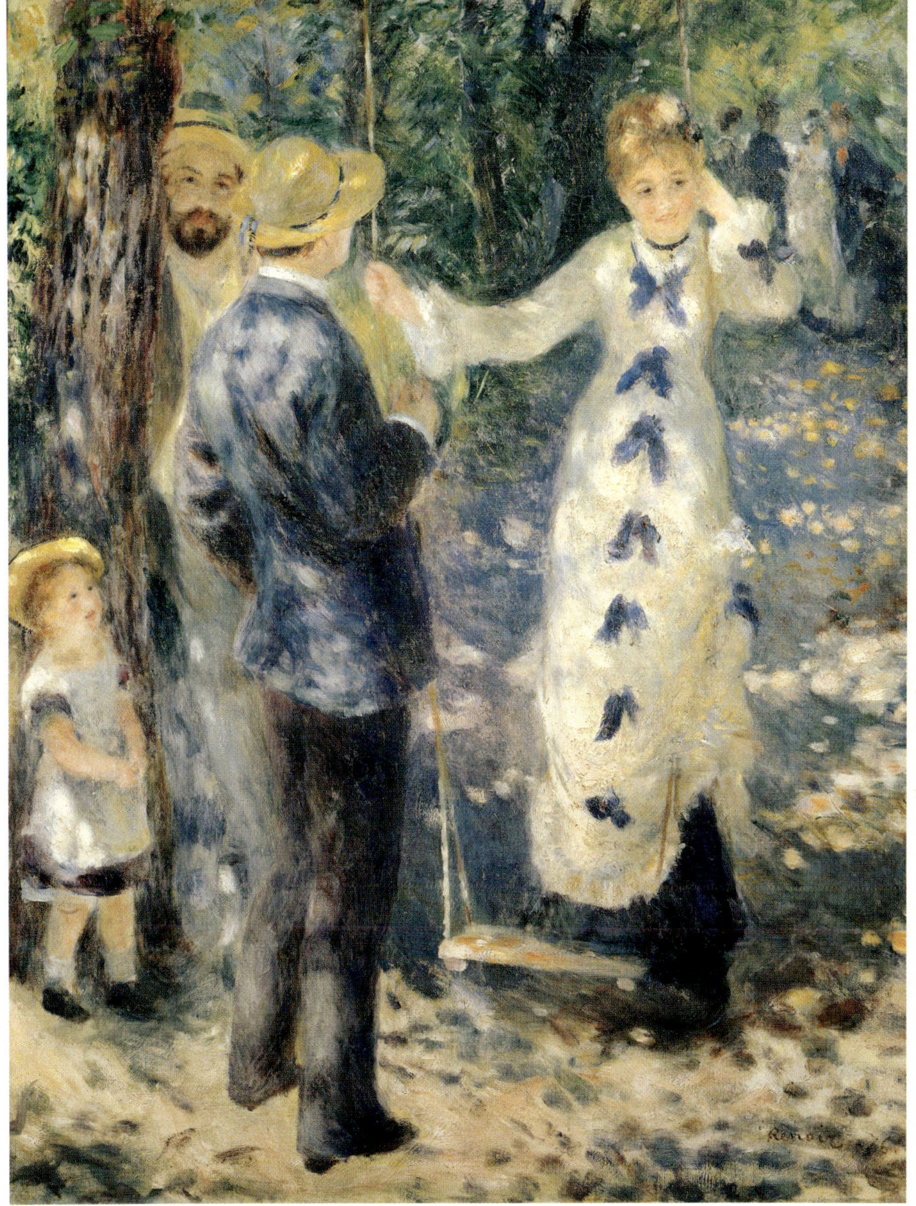

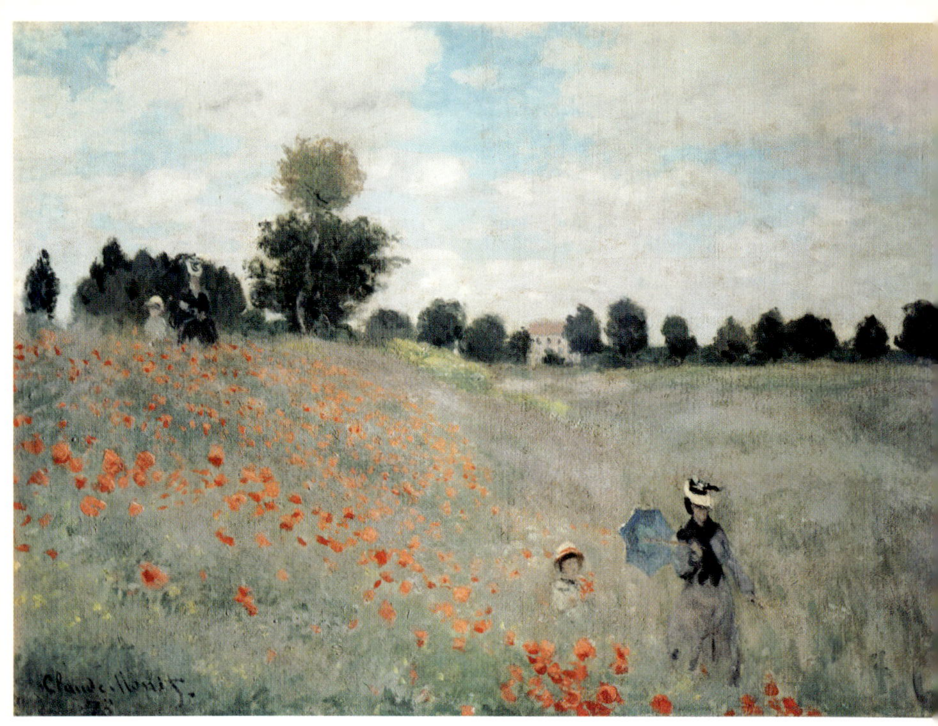

8. Claude Monet
Poppies, near Argenteuil, 1873

9. Pierre-Auguste Renoir
The Path in the Long Grass,
circa 1874

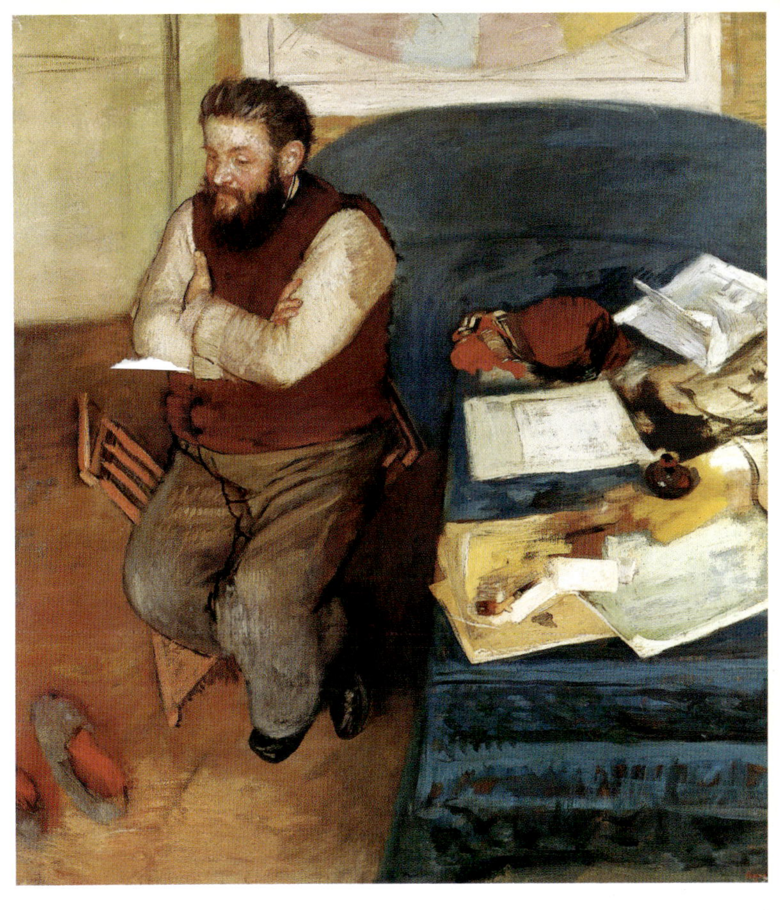

10. Édouard Manet
Portrait of Émile Zola, 1868

11. Edgar Degas
Portrait of Diego Martelli, 1879

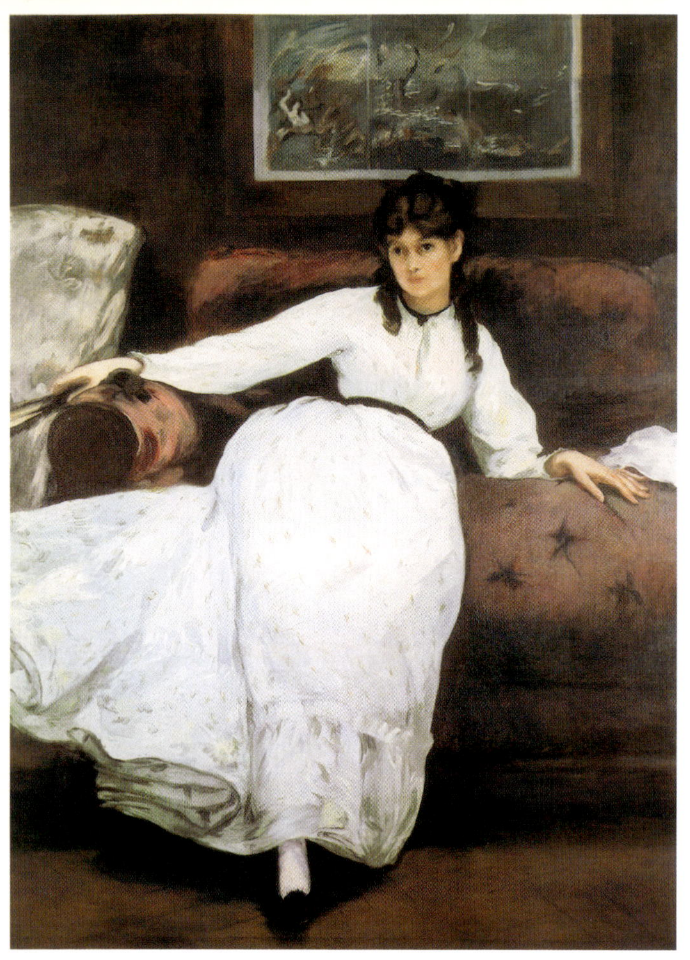

12. Édouard Manet
Repose. Portrait of Berthe Morisot, 1870

13. Édouard Manet
The Balcony, 1868-69

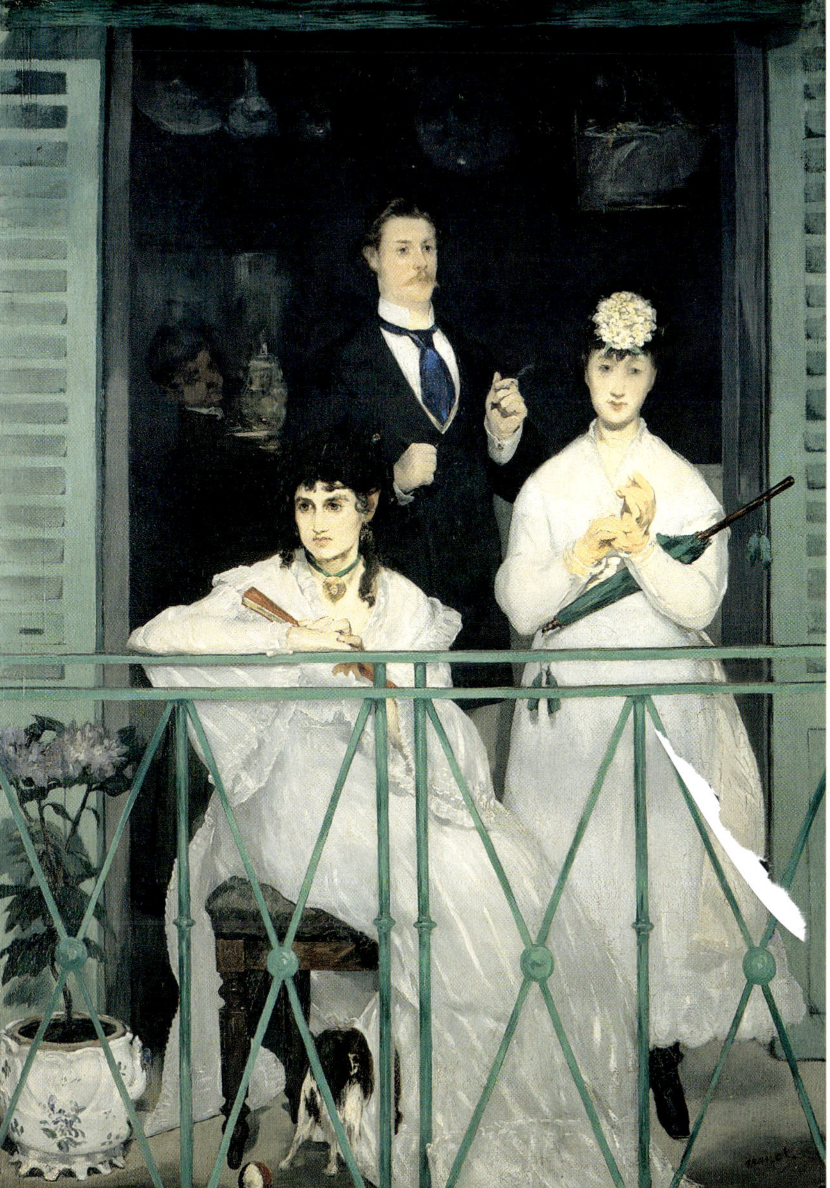

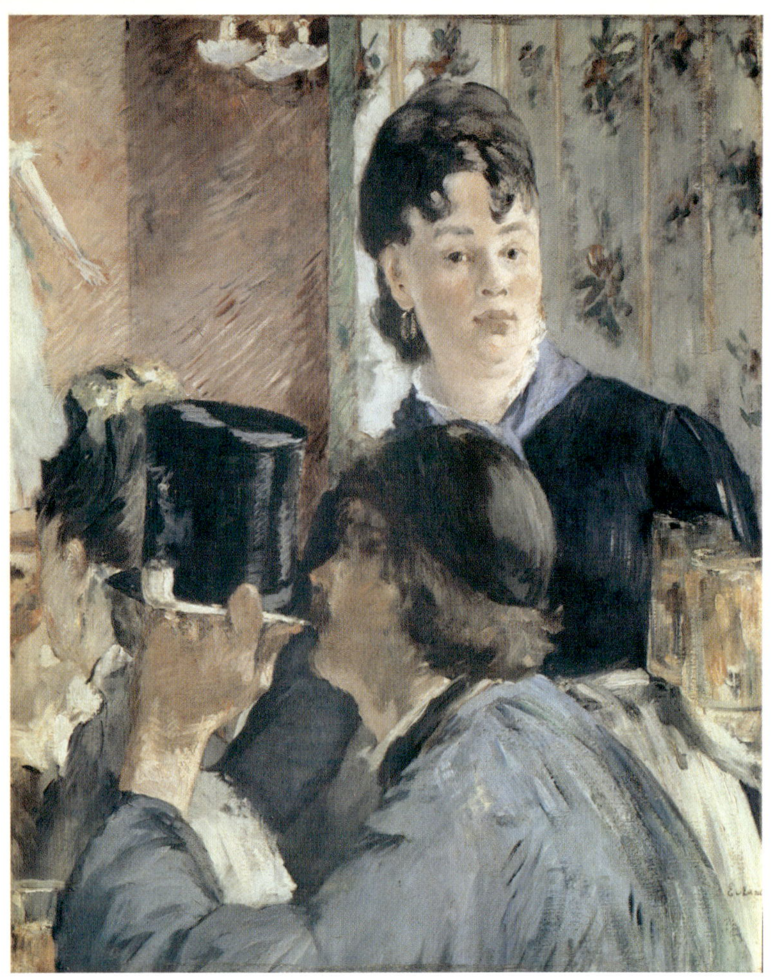

14. Édouard Manet
The Waitress, 1879

15. Pierre-Auguste Renoir
La Loge, 1874

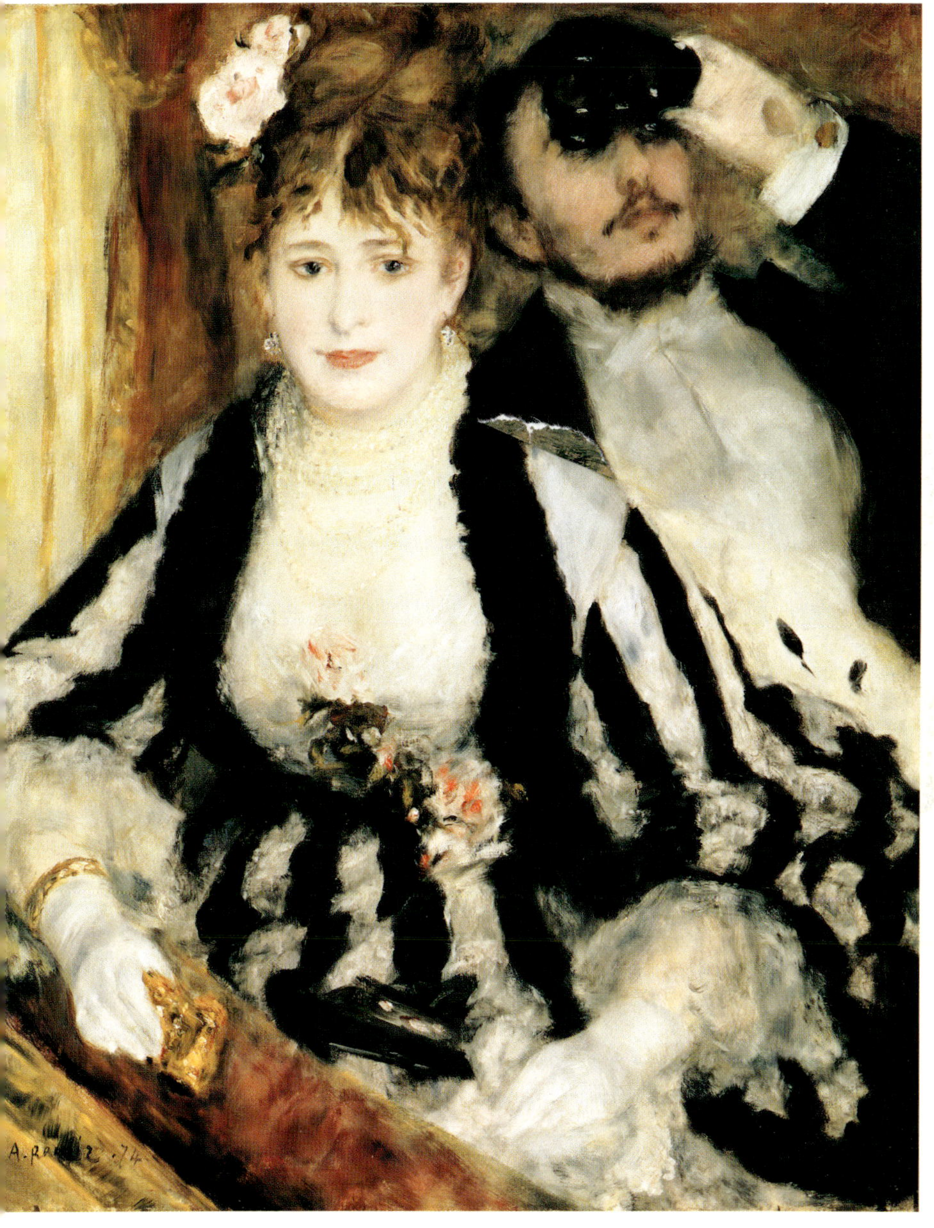

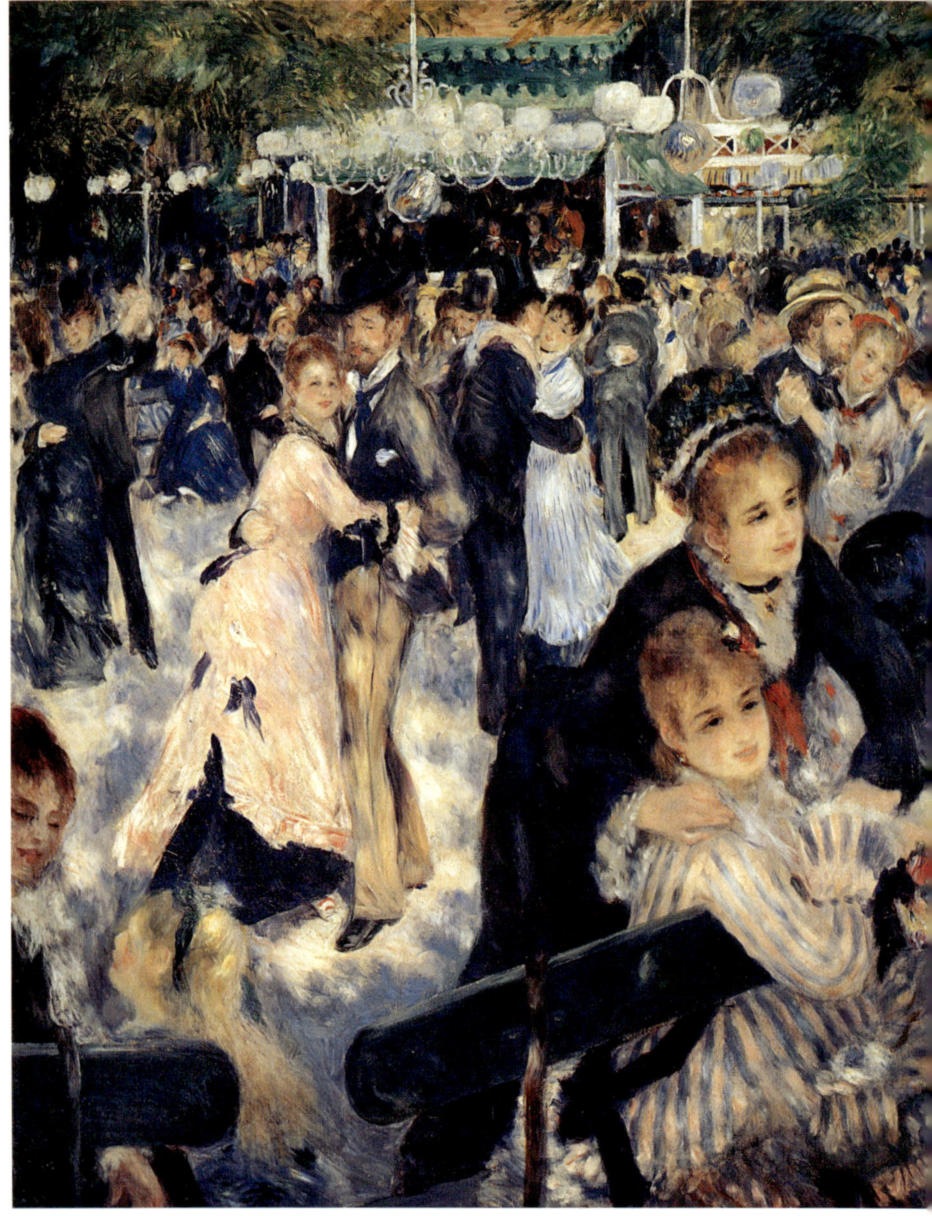

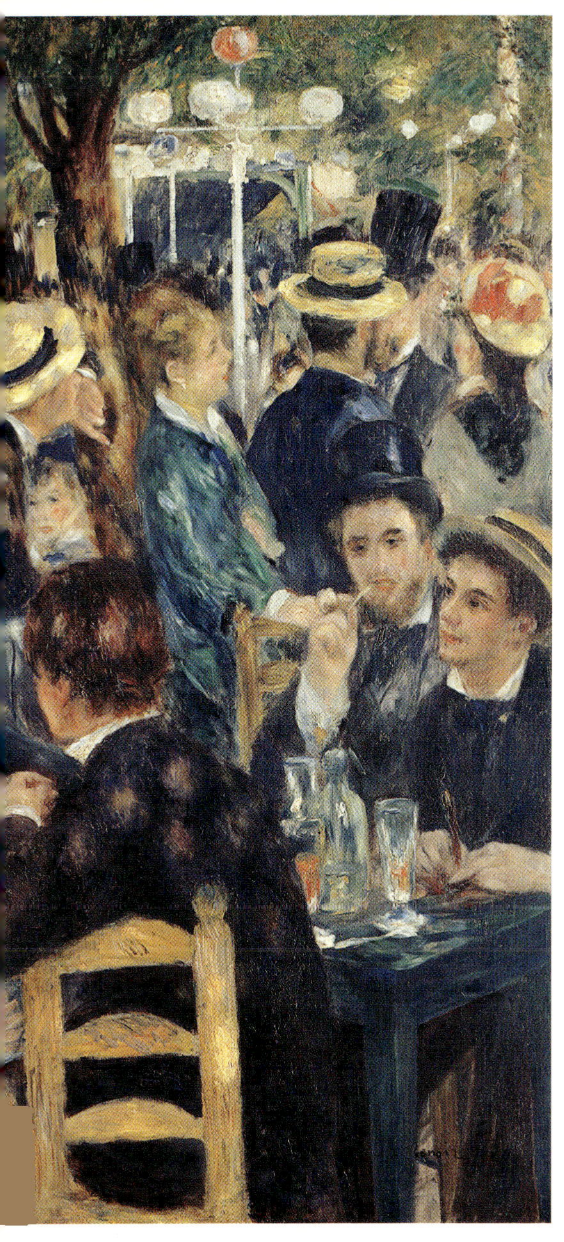

16. Pierre-Auguste Renoir
Bal au Moulin de la Galette,
1876

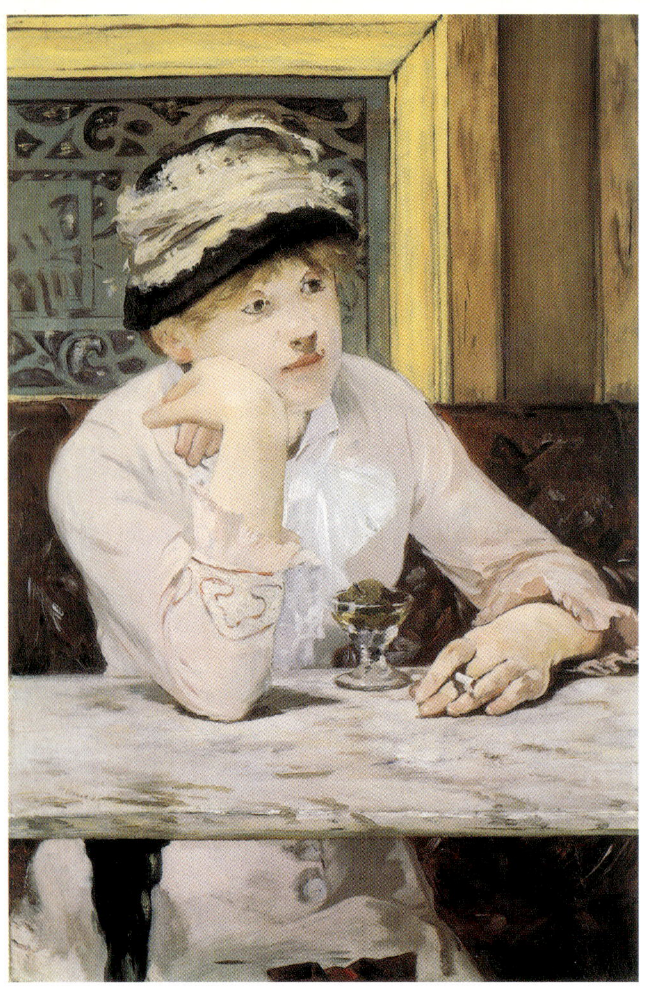

17. Édouard Manet
Plum Brandy, 1877-78

18. Edgar Degas
Absinthe (The Absinth Drinker), 1875-76

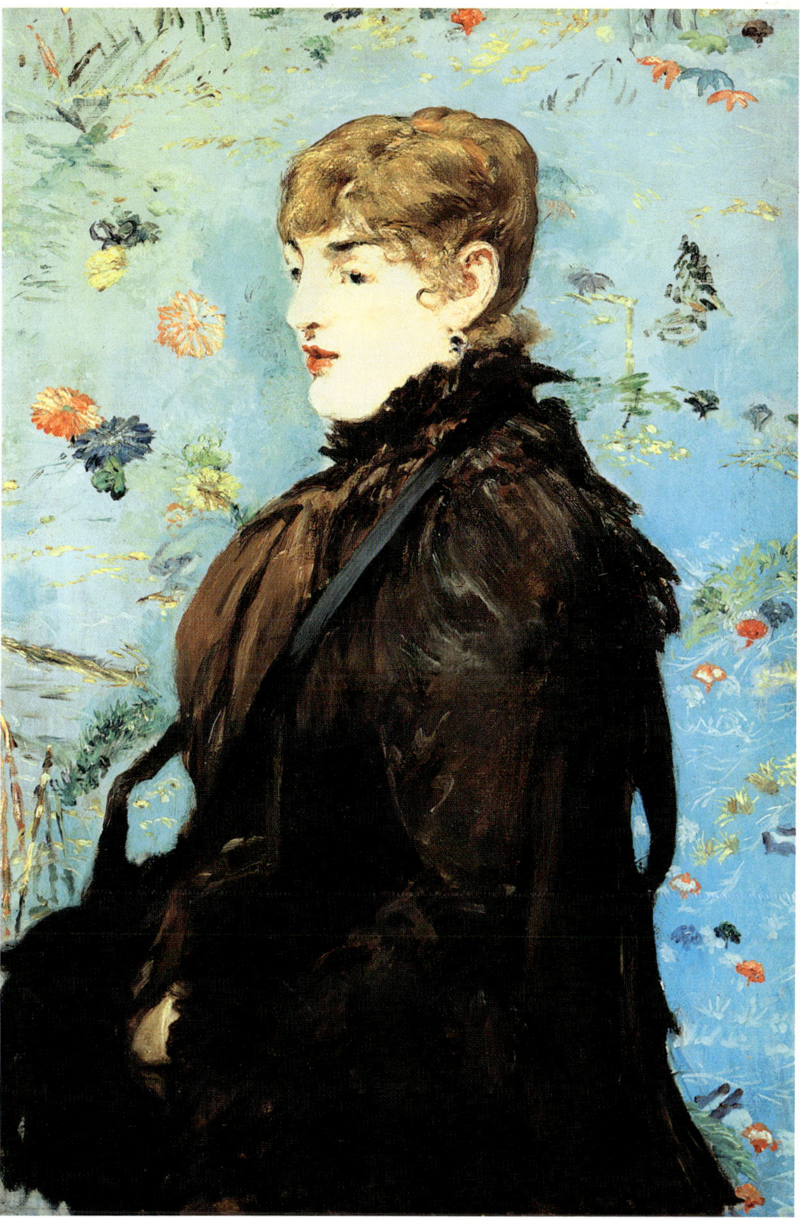

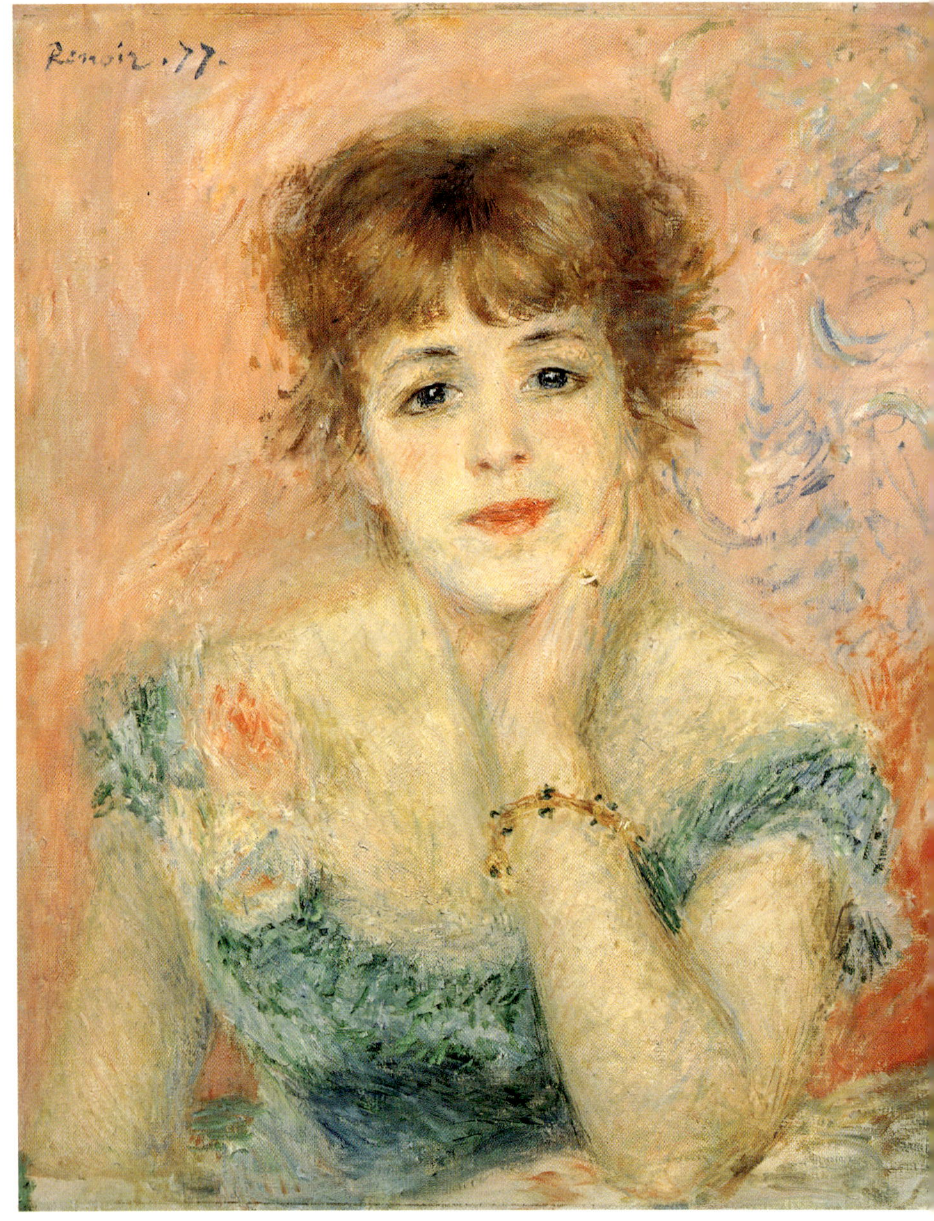
Renoir. 77.

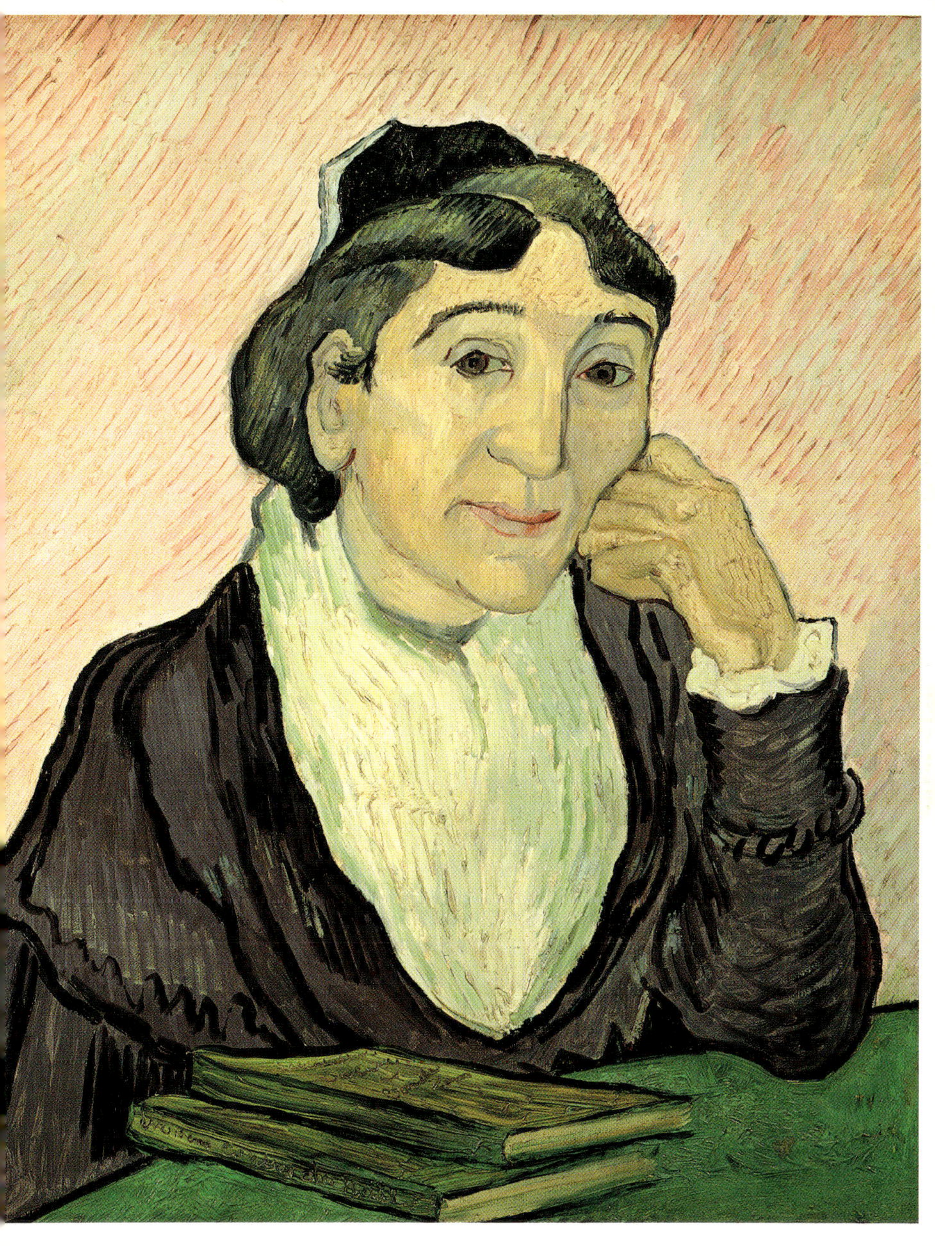

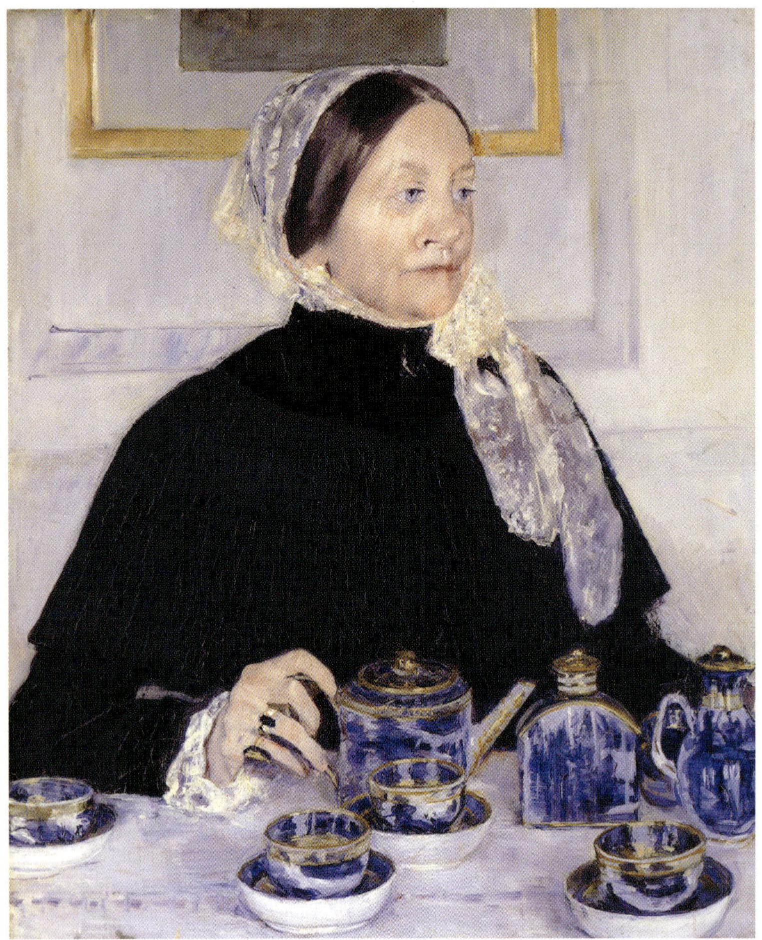

23. Mary Cassatt
Lady at the Tea Table, 1883-85

24. Vincent van Gogh
La Berceuse (Madame Roulin Rocking the Cradle), 1889

Following pages

25. Paul Cézanne
La Dame au livre, 1902-04

26. Paul Cézanne
Woman in Blue, *circa* 1904

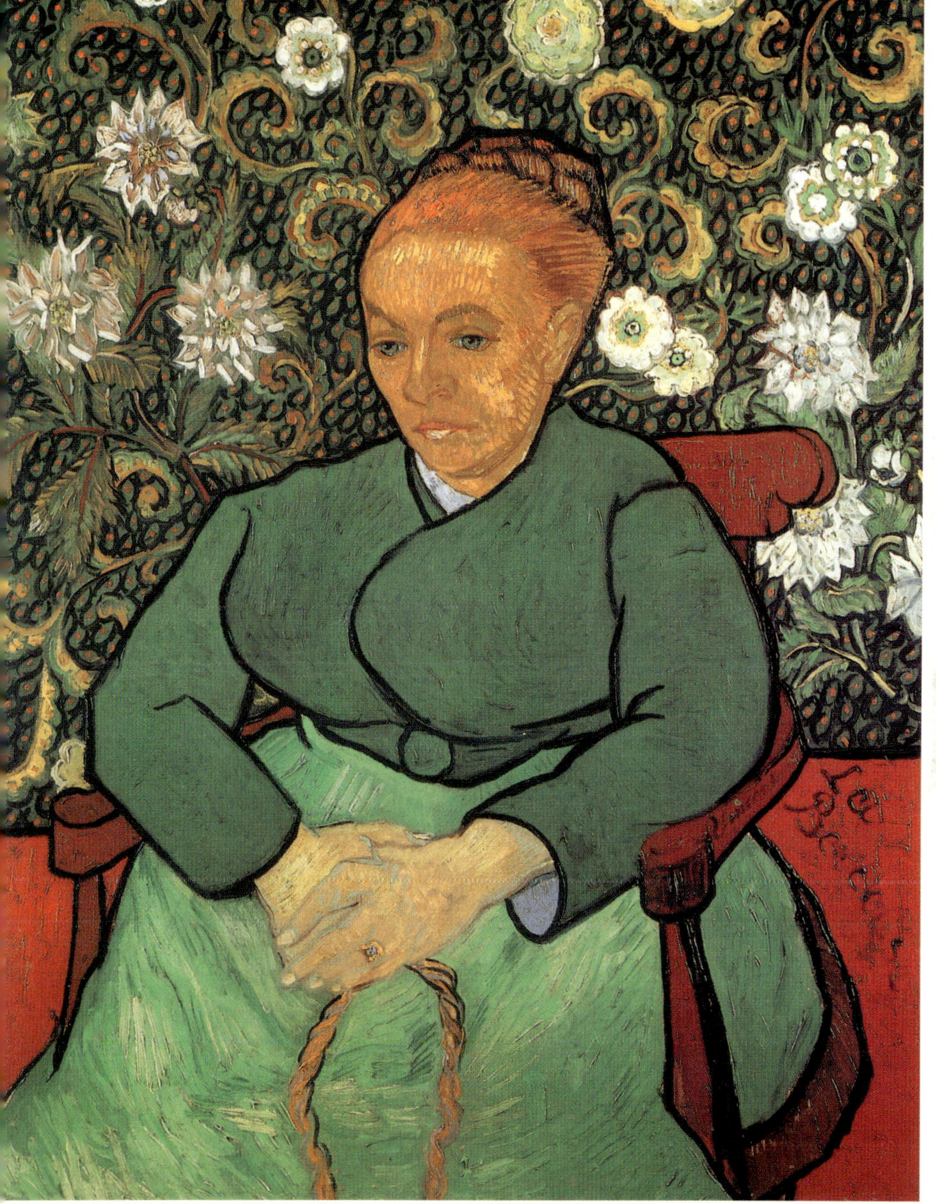
La

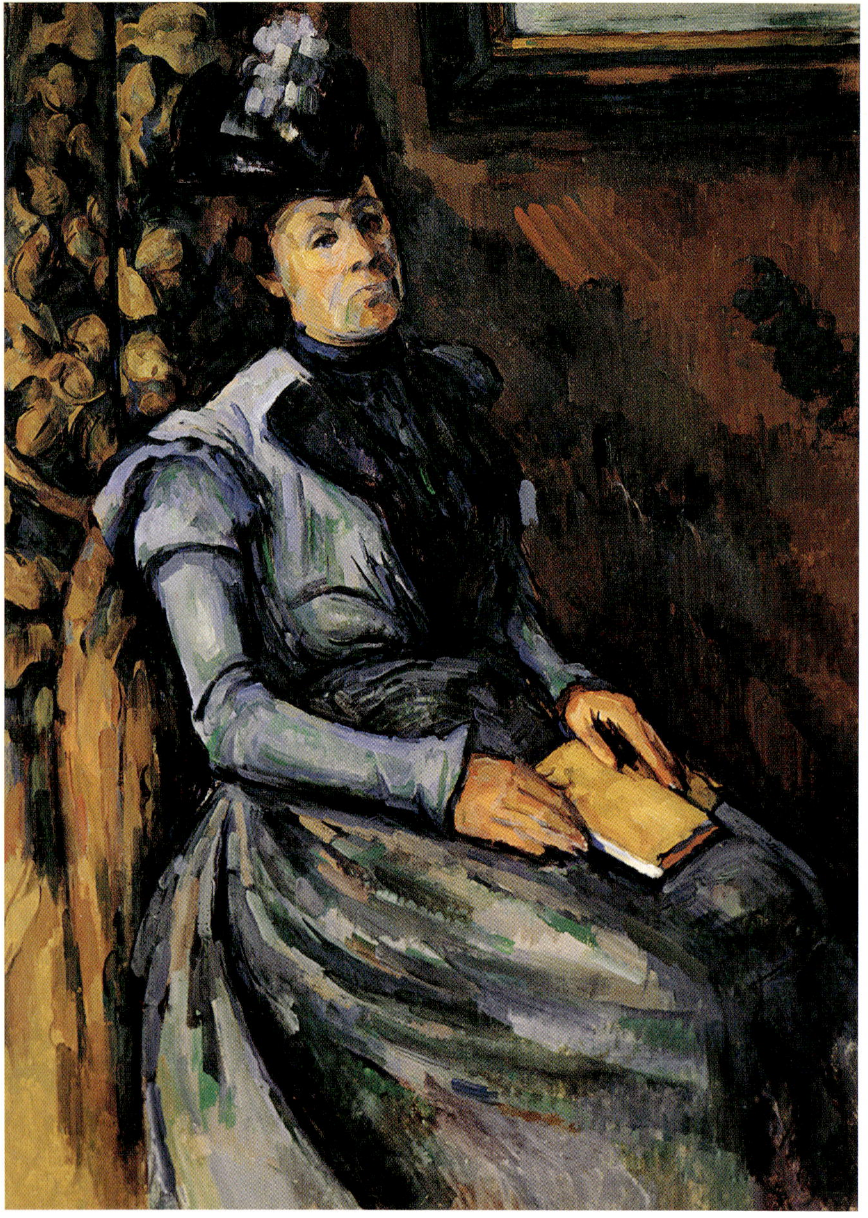

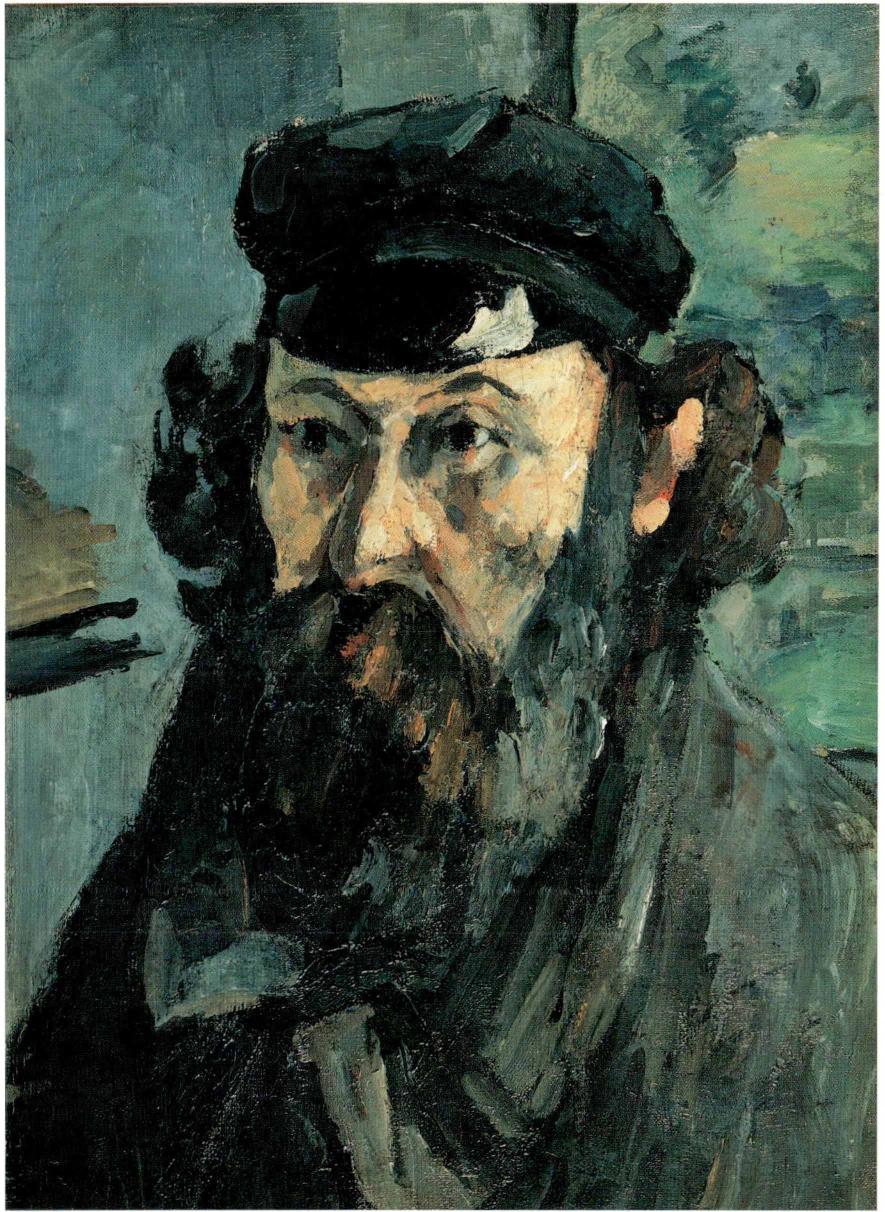

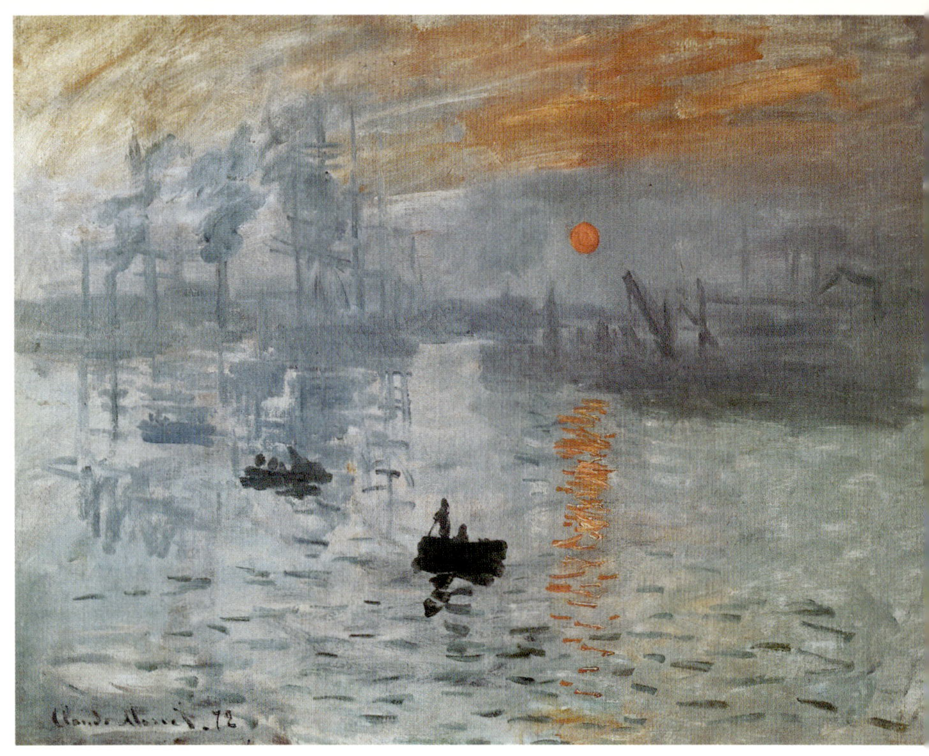

Previous pages
27. Camille Pissarro
Self-portrait, 1873

28. Paul Cézanne
Self-portrait with Beret, *circa* 1875

29. Claude Monet
Impression, soleil levant (Impression, Sunrise), 1872

30. Claude Monet
La Gare Saint-Lazare (Saint-Lazare Station), 1877

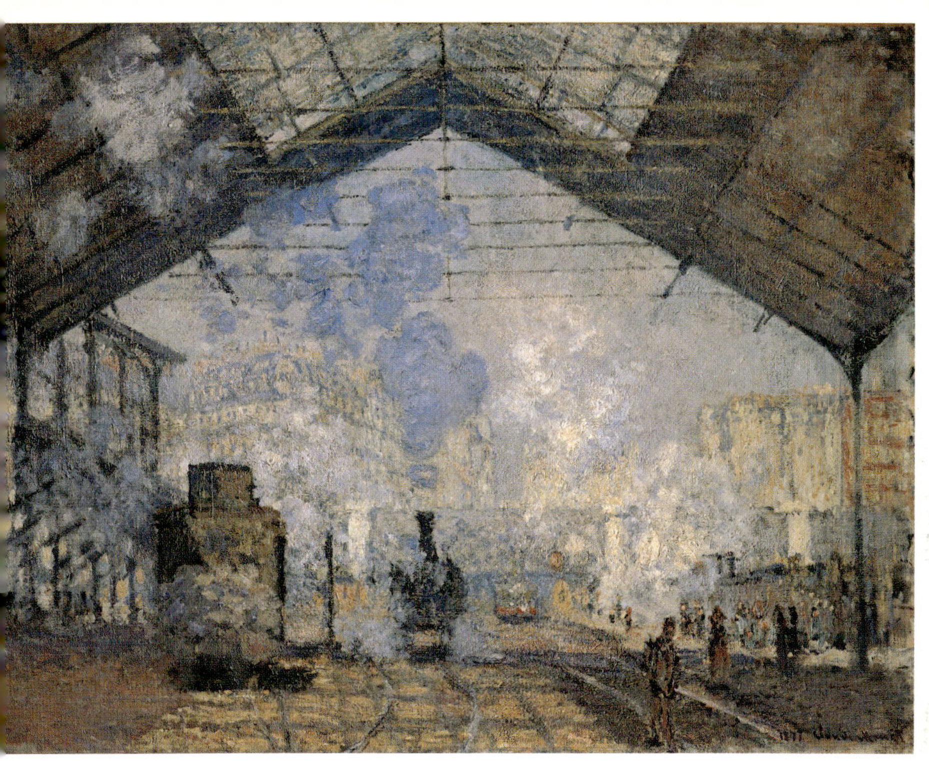

63

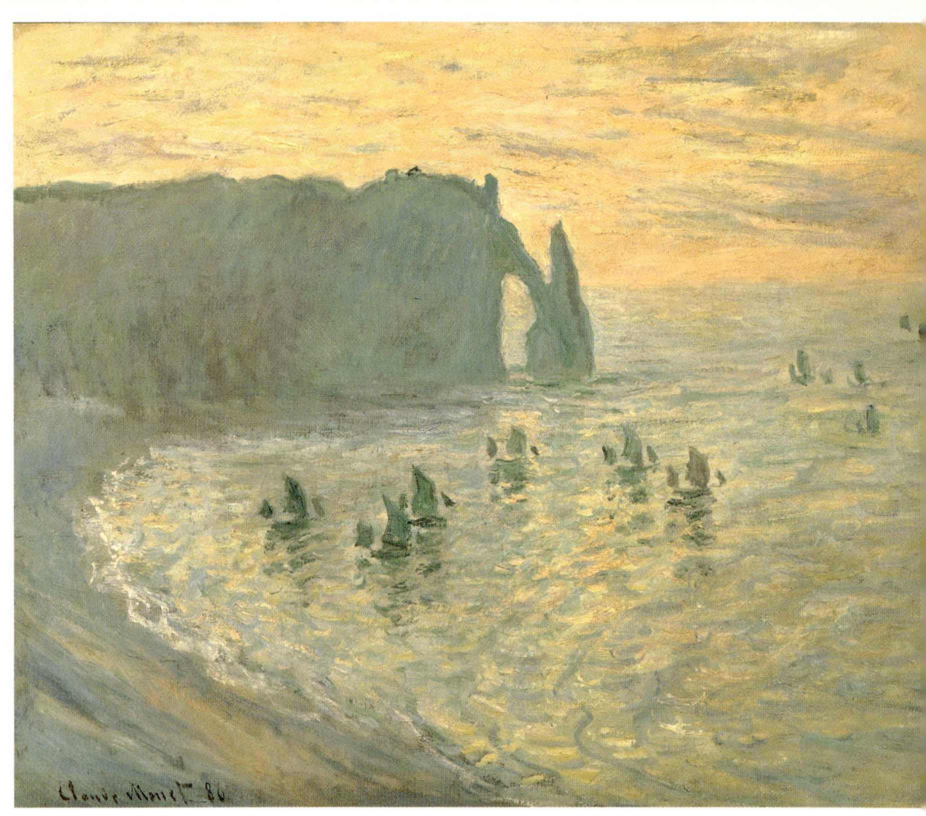
Claude Monet 86

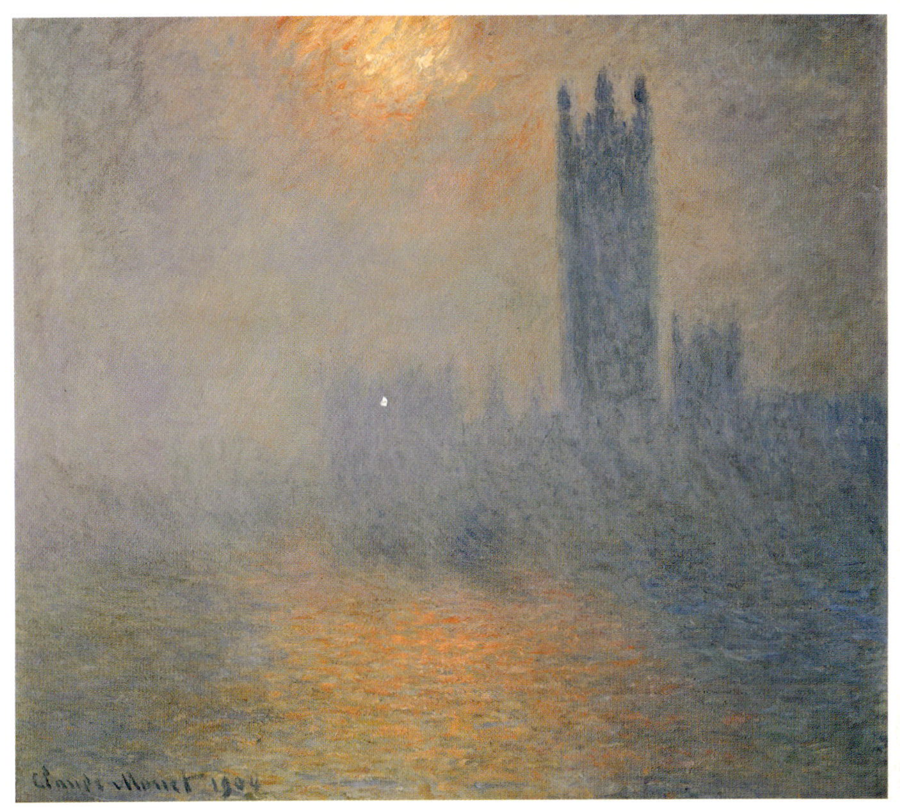

31. Claude Monet
Cliffs at Etretat, 1886

32. Claude Monet
Houses of Parliament, London, Sun Breaking Through the Fog, 1904

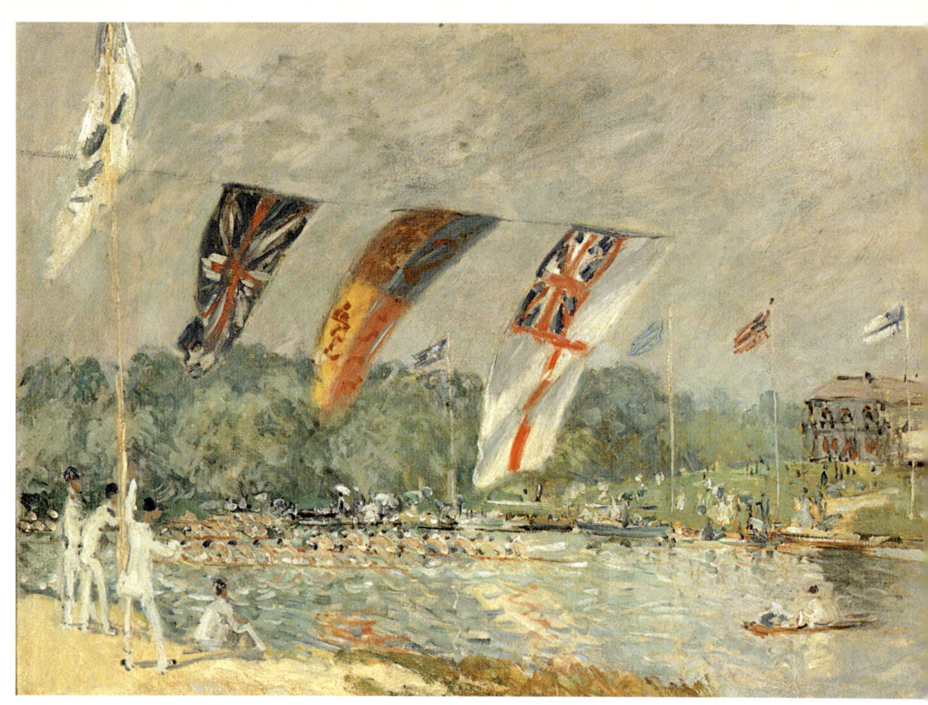

33. Alfred Sisley
Regatta at Molesey, 1874

34. Claude Monet
Rue Saint-Denis, Paris. Festivities of 30 June 1878, 1878

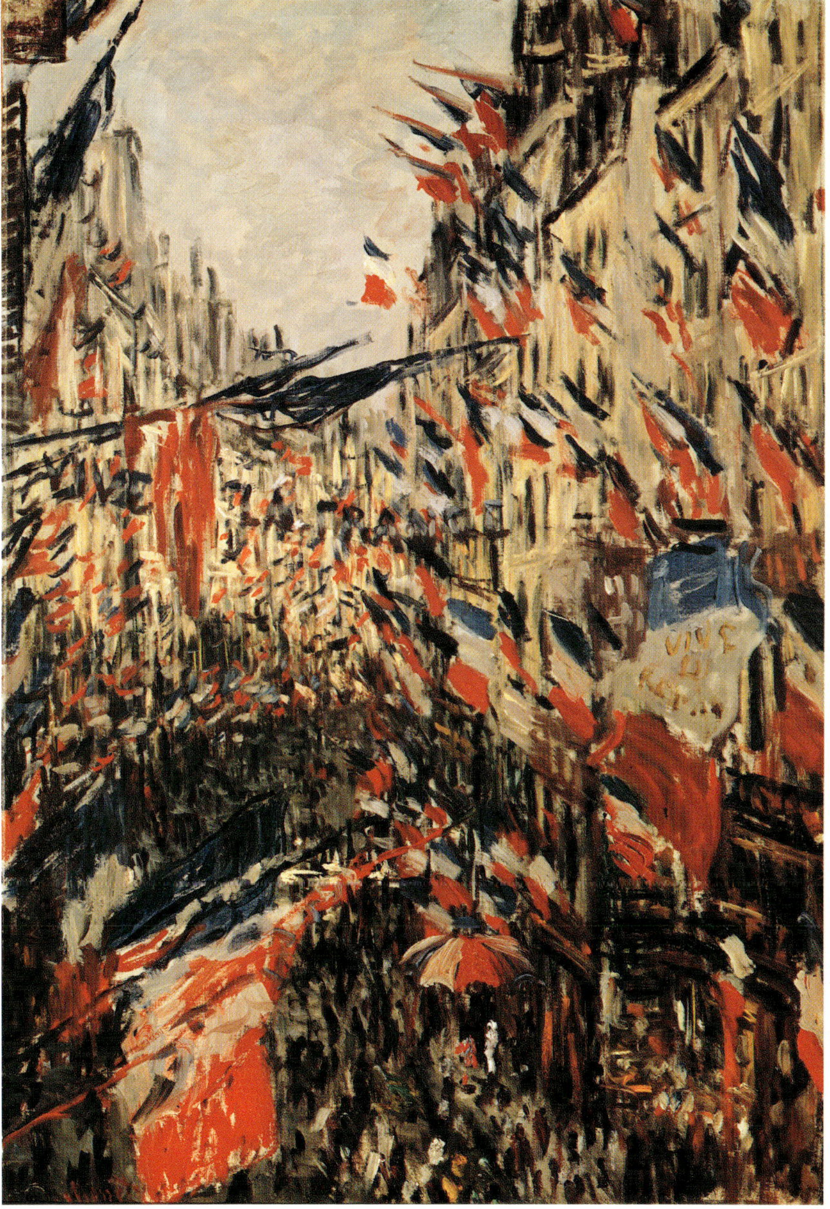

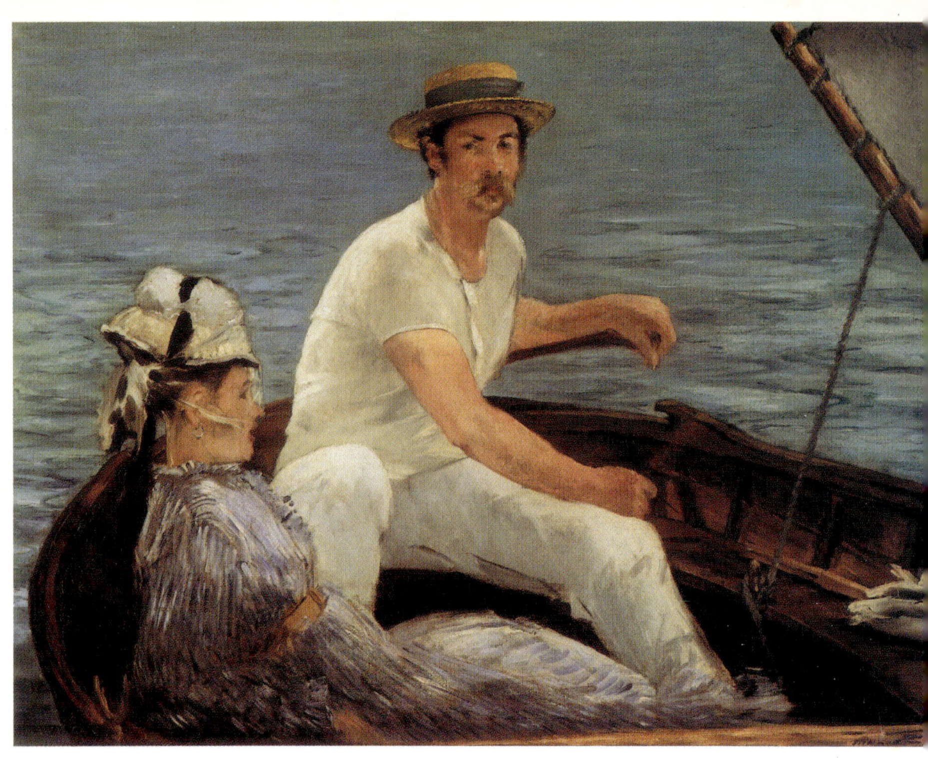

35. Édouard Manet
Boating, 1874

36. Édouard Manet
Chez le Père Lathuille, 1879

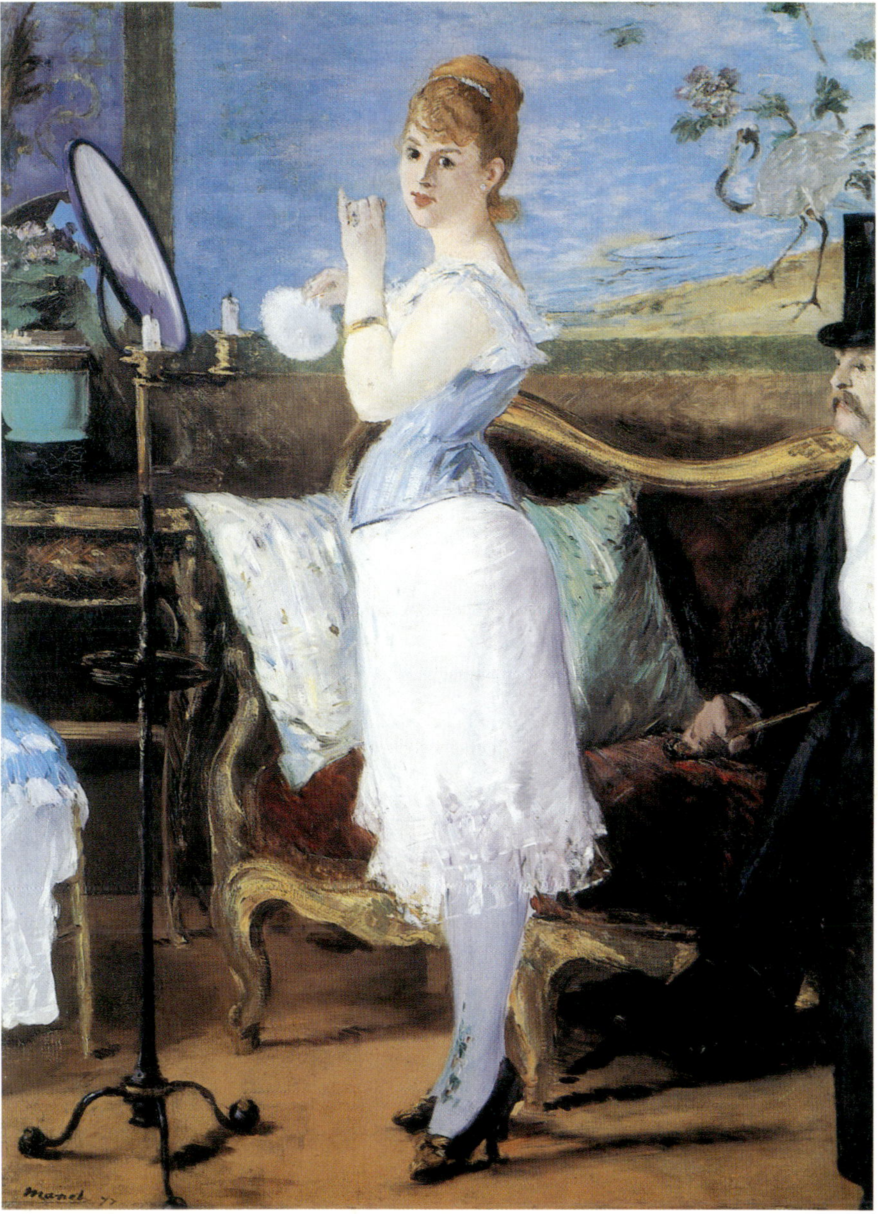
manet 77

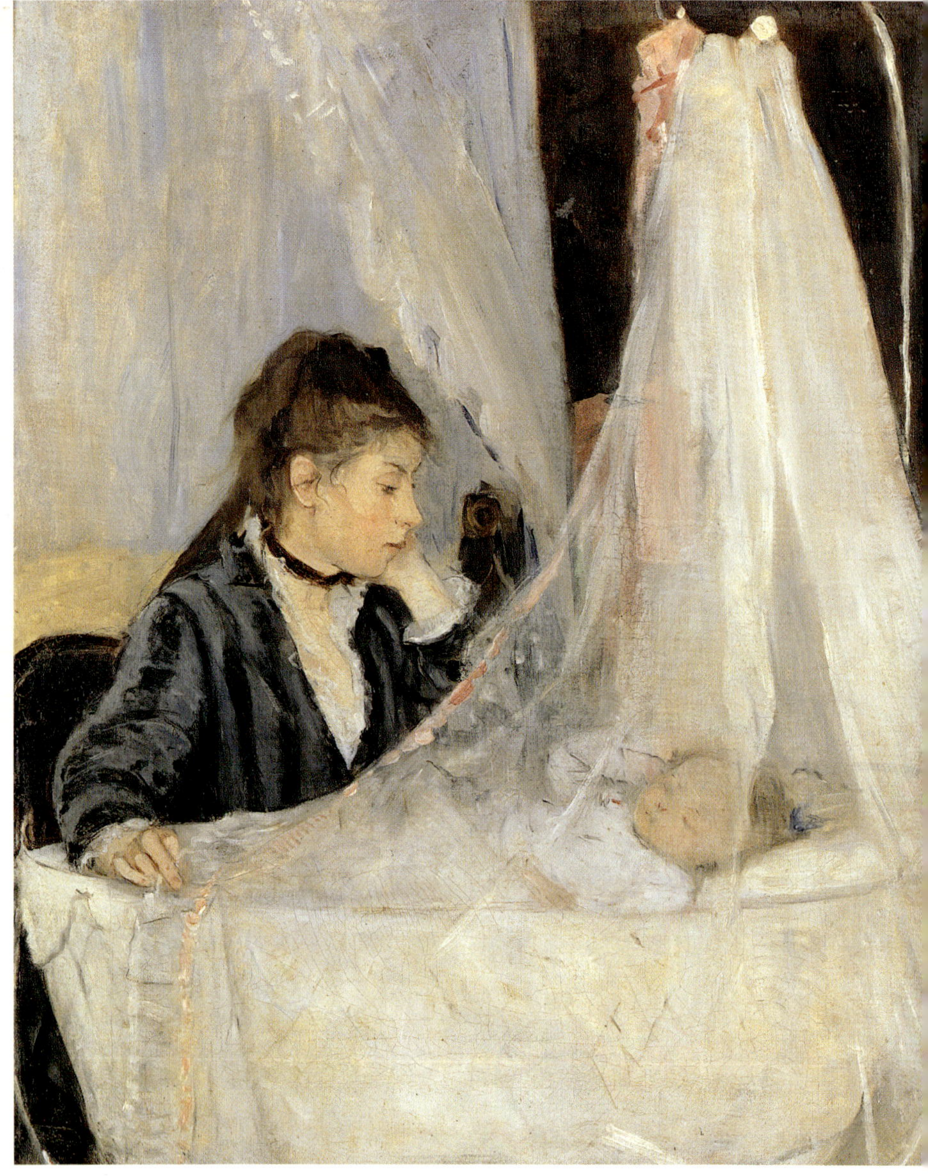

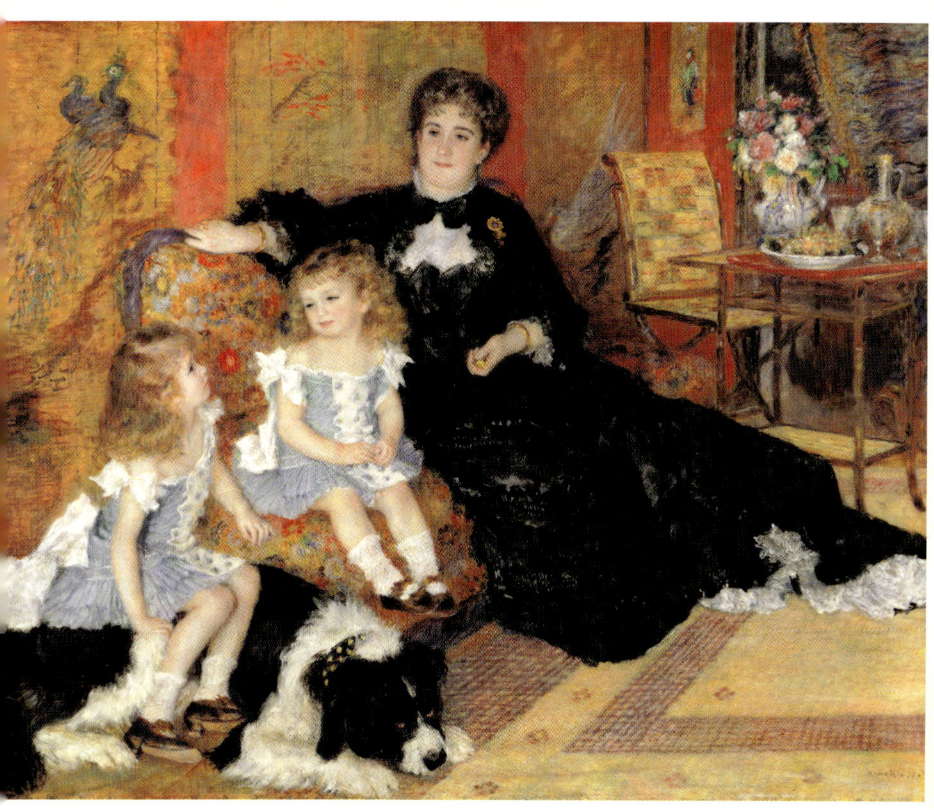

39. **Berthe Morisot**
The Cradle, 1872

40. **Pierre-Auguste Renoir**
Madame Georges Charpentier and her Children, 1878

Following pages
41. **Edgar Degas**
Miss La La at the Cirque Fernando, 1879

42. **Edgar Degas**
Dancer at the Photographer's, *circa* 1875

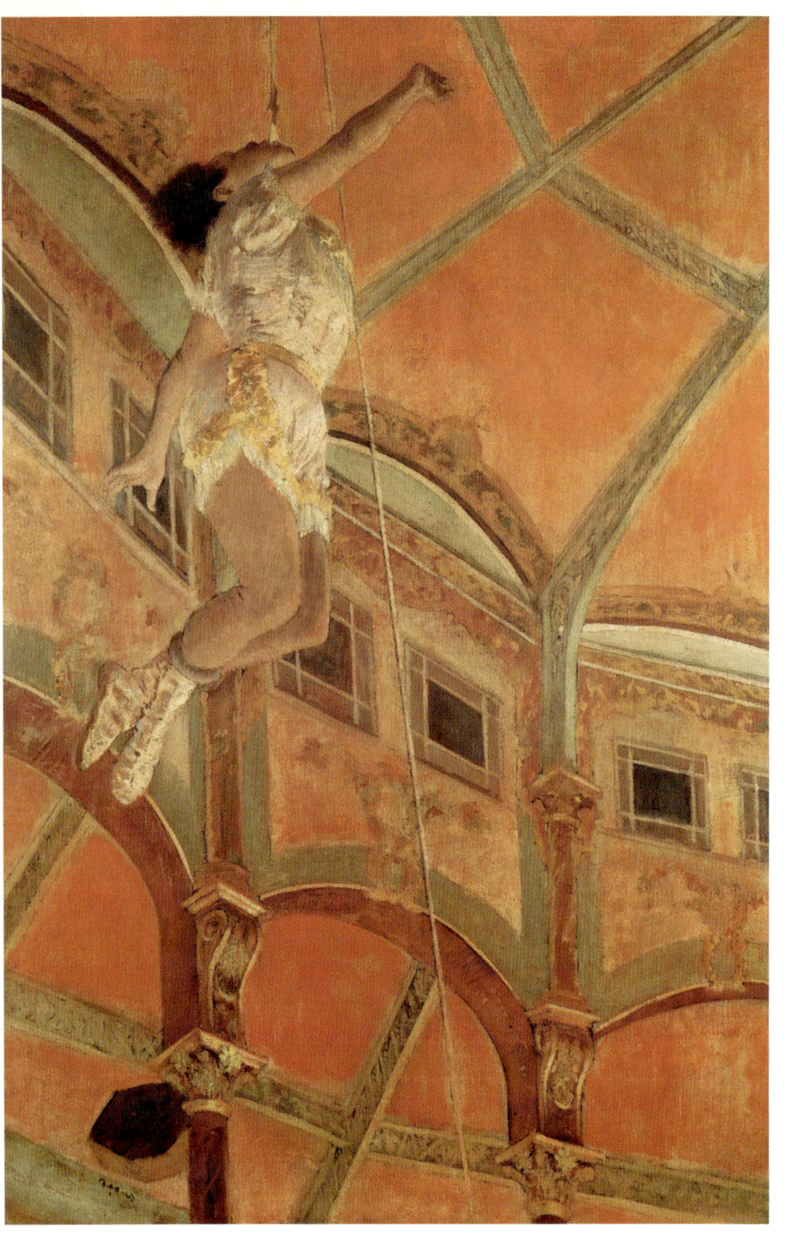

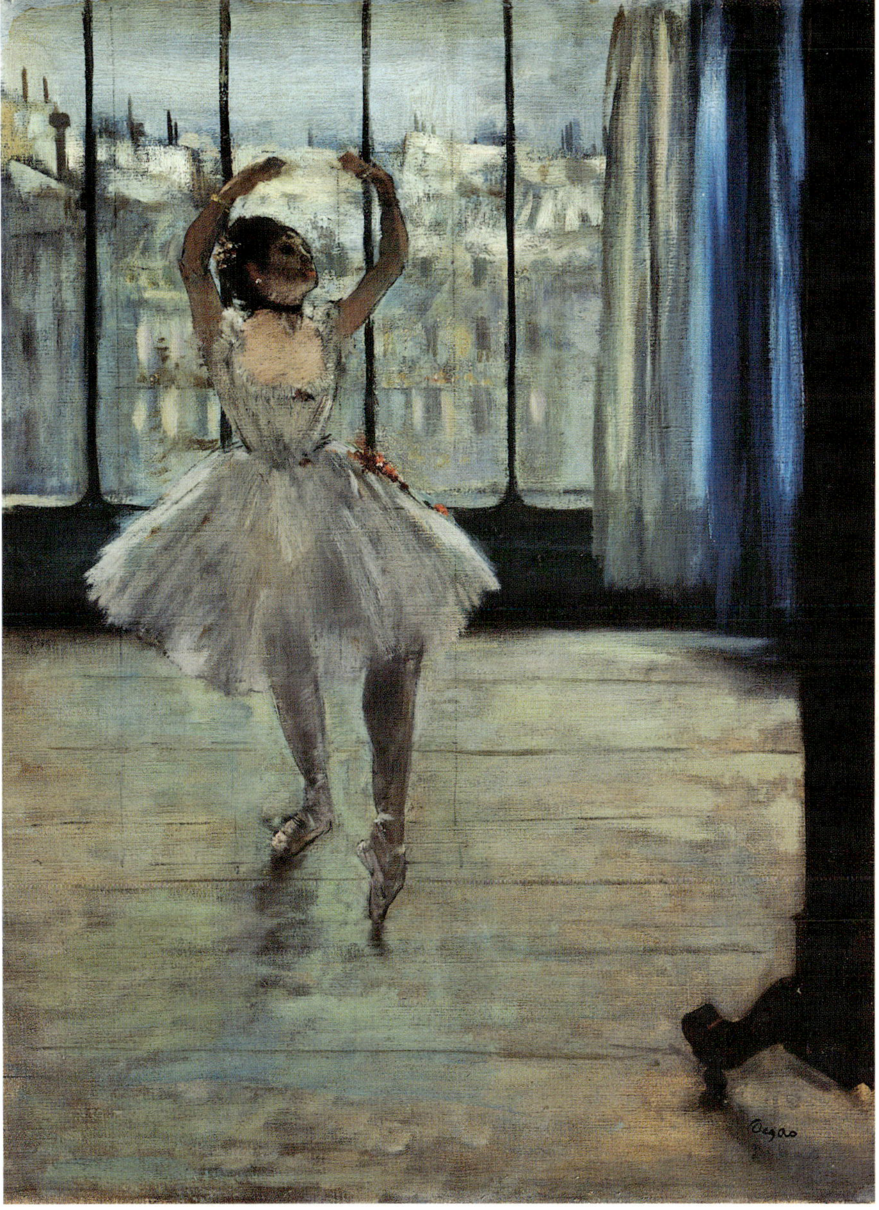
Degas

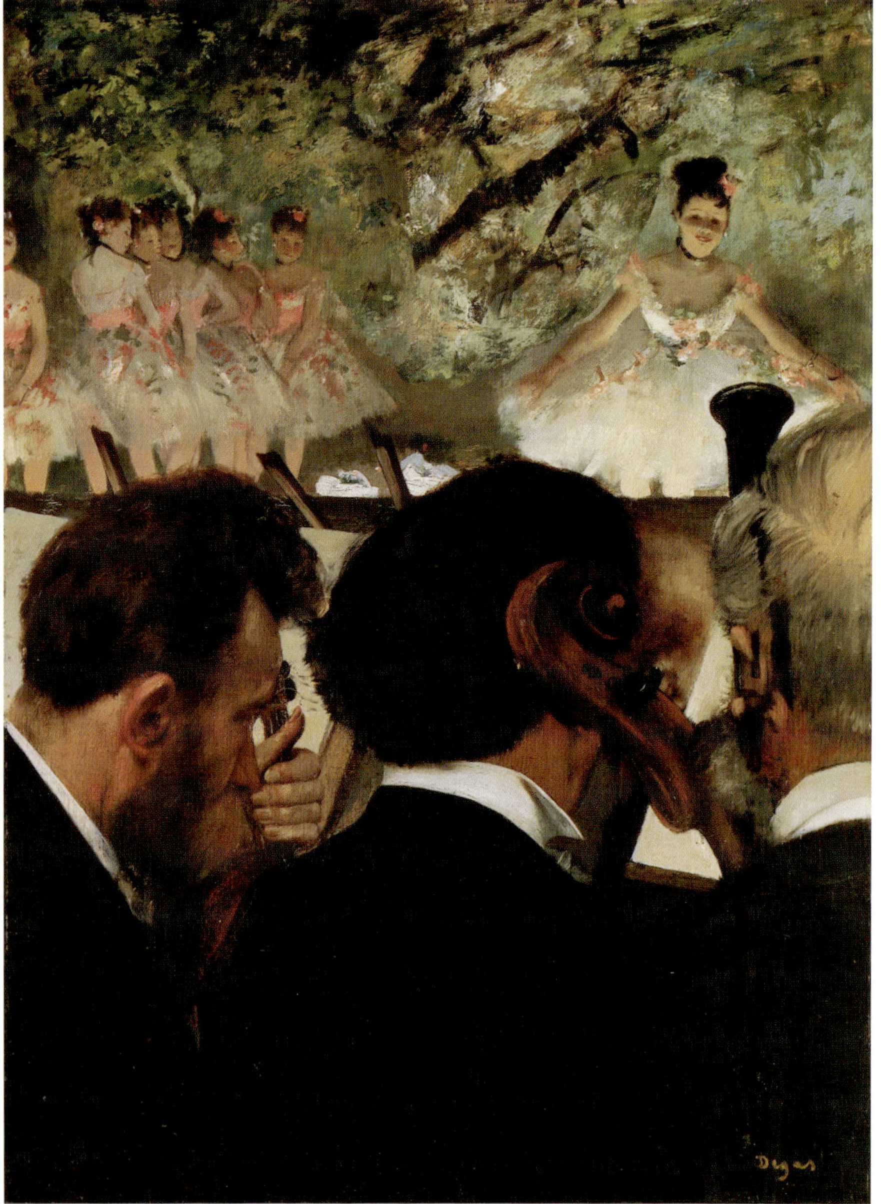
Degas

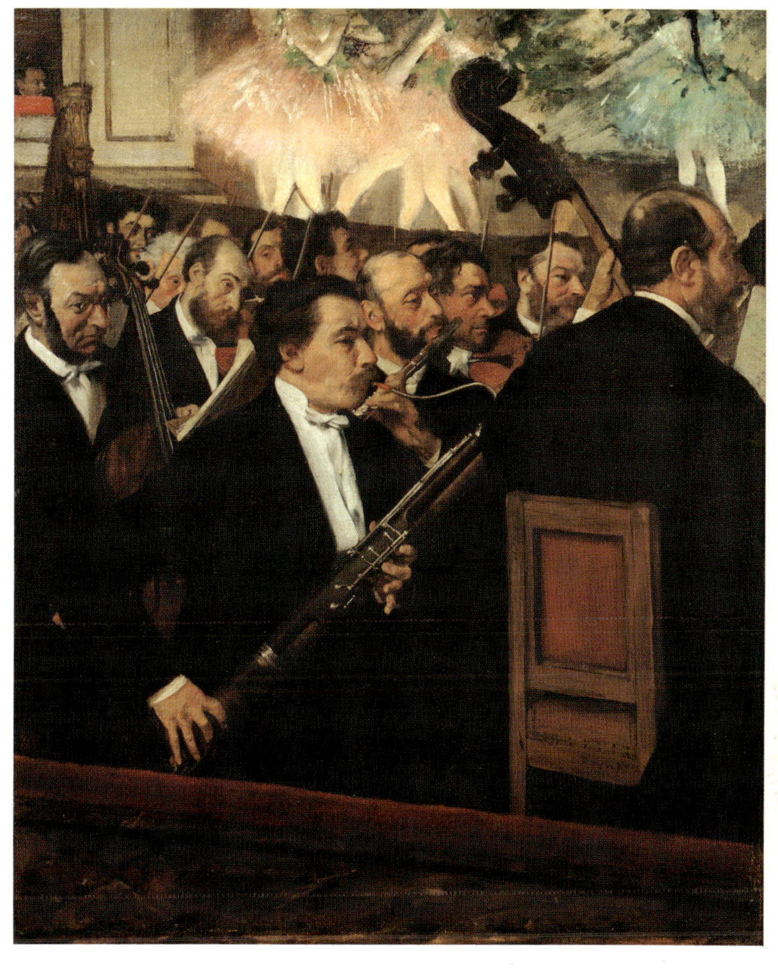

43. Edgar Degas
At Ballet, 1874-76

44. Edgar Degas
The Orchestra of the Opera, circa 1868

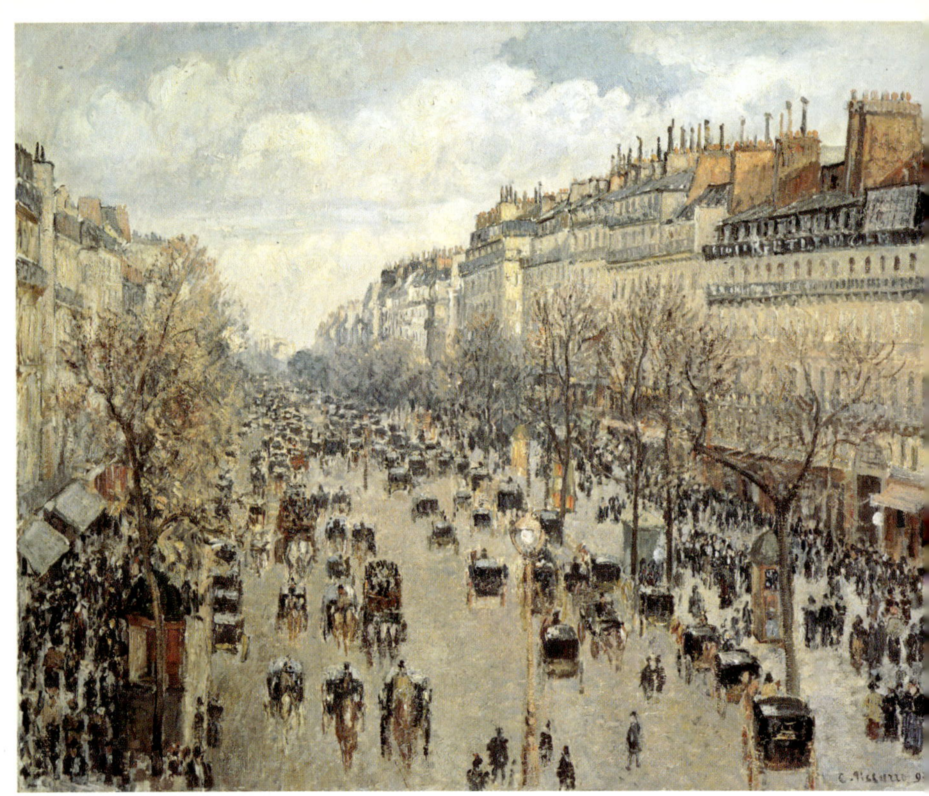

45. Camille Pissarro
Boulevard Montmartre in Paris. Sunny Afternoon, 1897

46. Camille Pissarro
Boïeldieu Bridge, Rouen, 1896

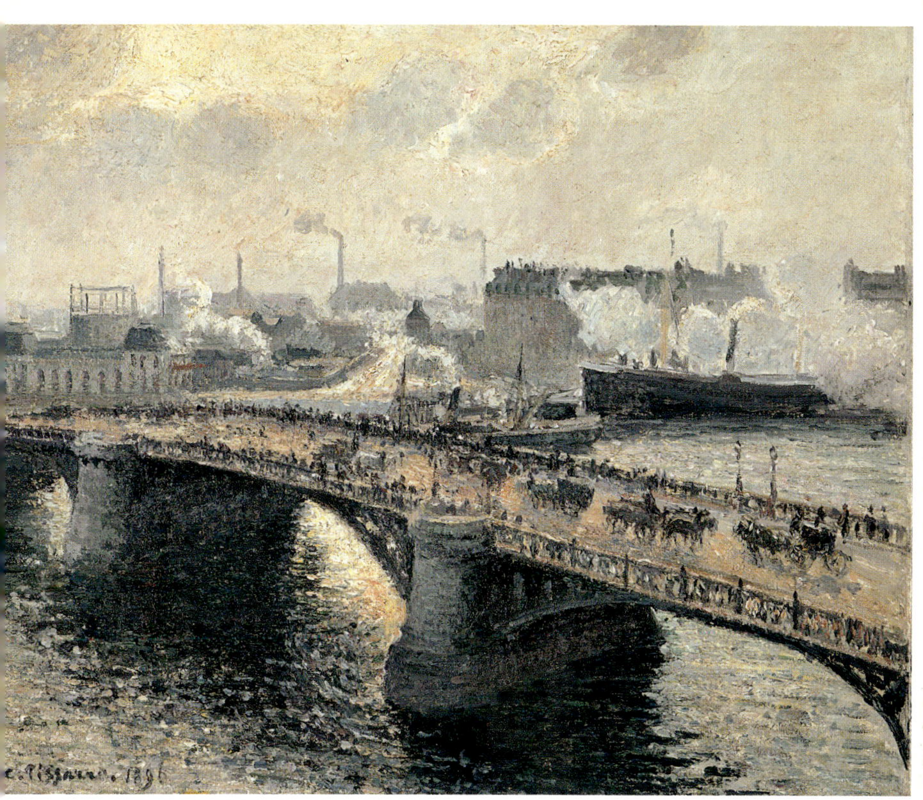
C. Pissarro. 1896

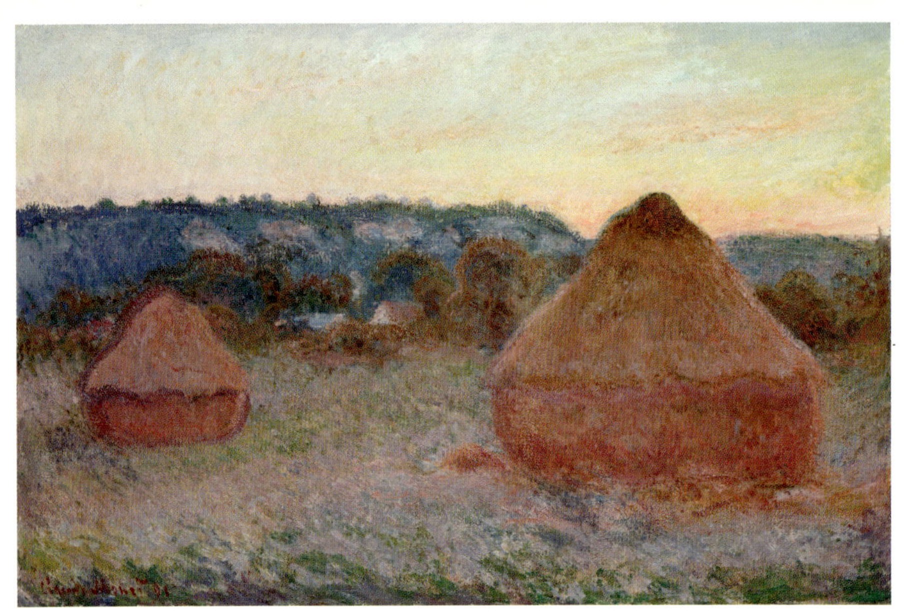

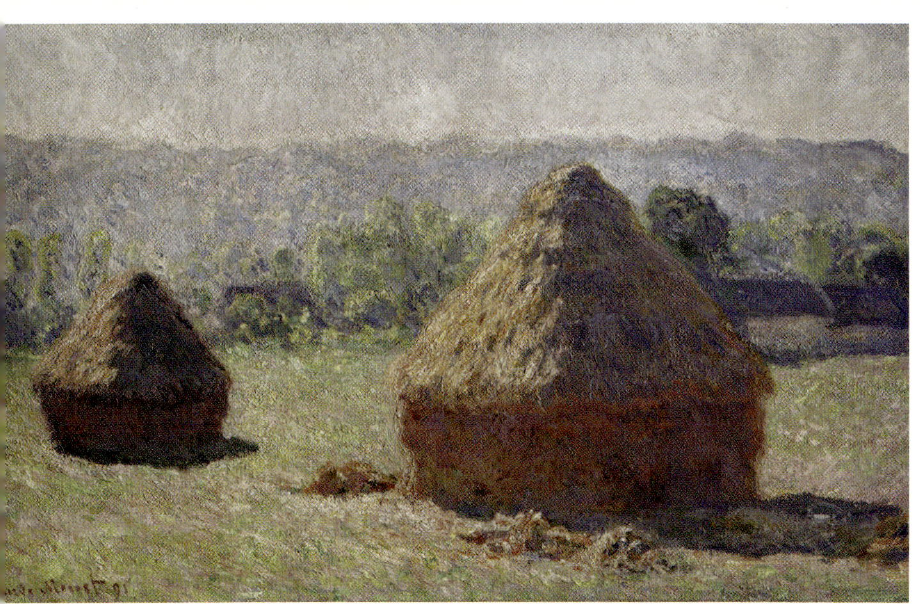

47. Claude Monet
Stacks of Wheat (End of Day, Autumn), 1890-91

48. Claude Monet
Stacks of Wheat (Late Summer), 1891

Following pages
49. Claude Monet
Rouen Cathedral, Morning Sun, 1894

50. Claude Monet
Rouen Cathedral, Midday, 1894

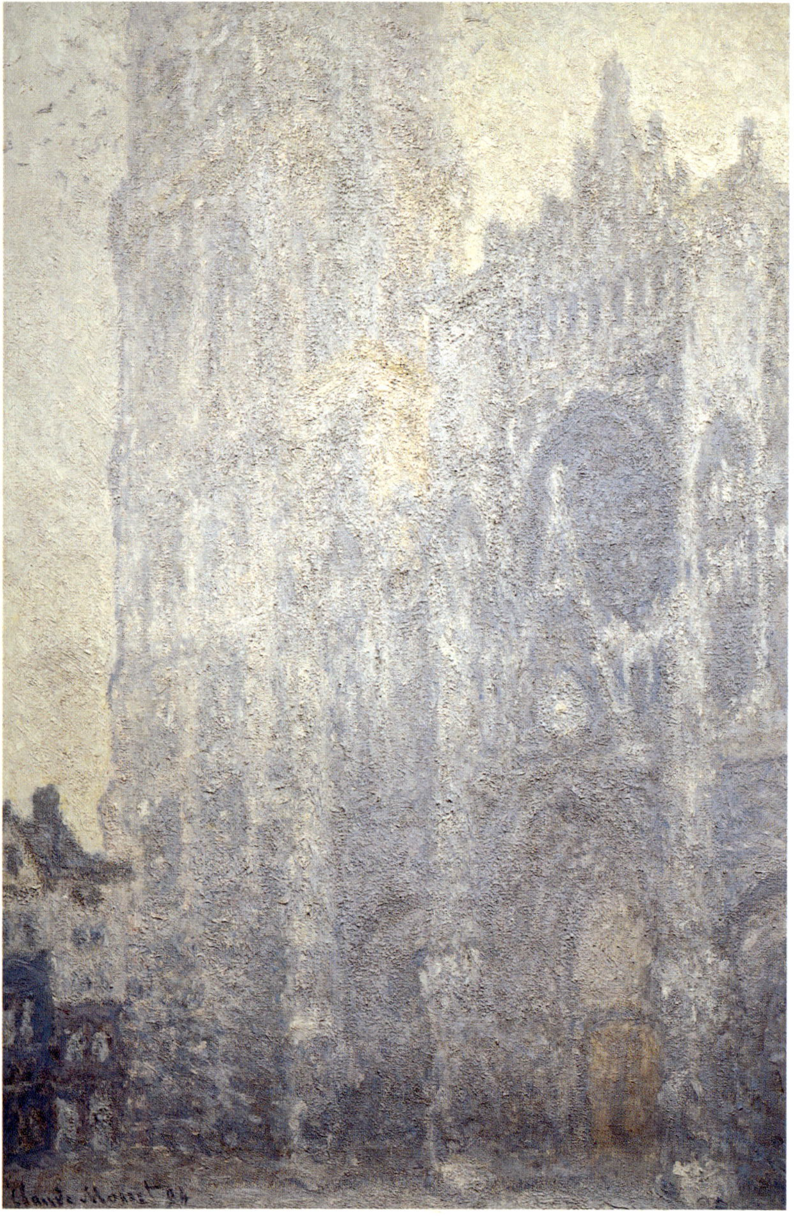

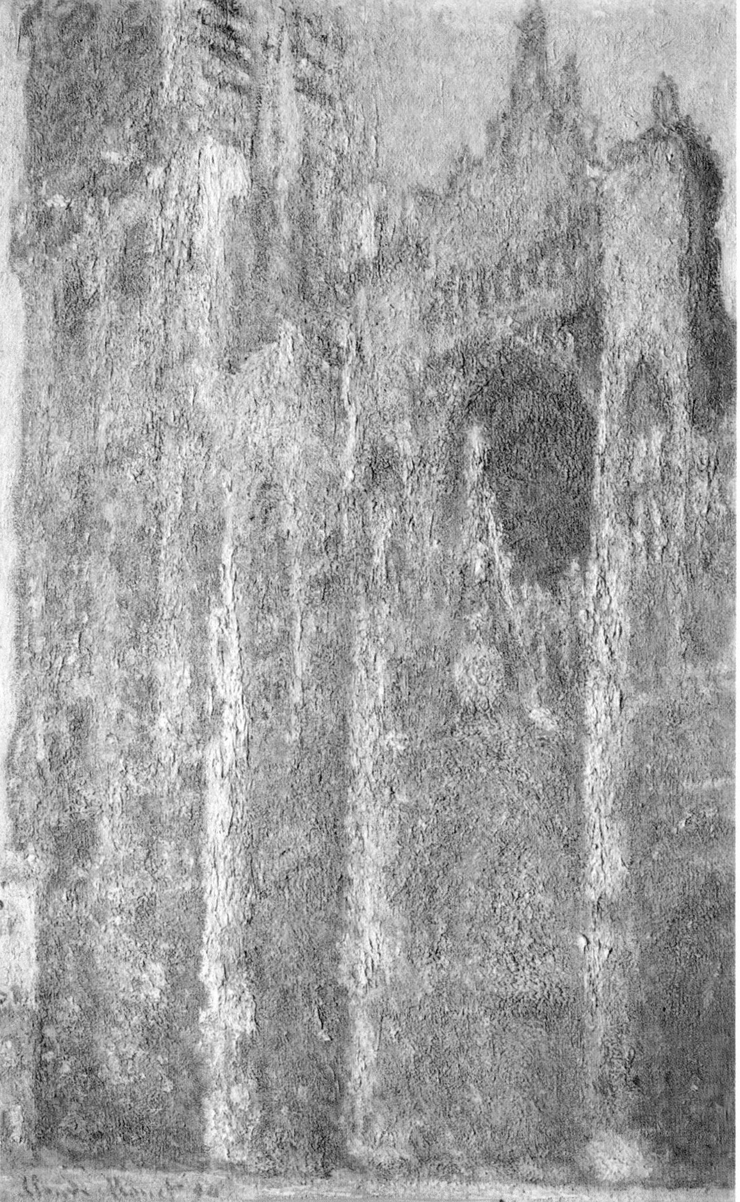

Appendix

Catalogue of the Works

1. Claude Monet
Garden at Sainte-Adresse, 1867
Oil on canvas, 98.1 x 129.9 cm
The Metropolitan Museum of Art, New York, Purchase, special contributions and funds given or bequeathed by friends of the Museum, 1967

2. Édouard Manet
Olympia, 1863
Oil on canvas, 130.5 x 190 cm
Musée d'Orsay, Paris

3. Édouard Manet
Le Déjeuner sur l'Herbe (The Luncheon on the Grass), 1863
Oil on canvas, 208 x 264 cm
Musée d'Orsay, Paris

4. Silvestro Lega
After Dinner (The Pergola), 1868
Oil on canvas, 75 x 93.5 cm
Pinacoteca di Brera, Milan

5. Claude Monet
Women in the Garden, 1867
Oil on canvas, 255 x 205 cm
Musée d'Orsay, Paris

6. Pierre-Auguste Renoir
The Pergola, 1876
Oil on canvas, 81 x 65 cm
Pushkin Museum, Moscow

7. Pierre-Auguste Renoir
The Swing, 1876
Oil on canvas, 92 x 73 cm
Musée d'Orsay, Paris

8. Claude Monet
Poppies, near Argenteuil, 1873
Oil on canvas, 50 x 65 cm
Musée d'Orsay, Paris

9. Pierre-Auguste Renoir
The Path in the Long Grass, *circa* 1874
Oil on canvas, 60 x 74 cm
Musée d'Orsay, Paris

10. Édouard Manet
Portrait of Émile Zola, 1868
Oil on canvas, 146 x 114 cm
Musée d'Orsay, Paris

11. Edgar Degas
Portrait of Diego Martelli, 1879
Oil on canvas, 110 x 100 cm
National Gallery of Scotland, Edinburgh

12. Édouard Manet
Repose. Portrait of Berthe Morisot, 1870
Oil on canvas, 148 x 113 cm
Museum of Art, Providence

13. Édouard Manet
The Balcony, 1868-69
Oil on canvas, 169 x 125 cm
Musée d'Orsay, Paris

14. Édouard Manet
The Waitress, 1879
Oil on canvas, 77.5 x 65 cm
Musée d'Orsay, Paris

15. Pierre-Auguste Renoir
La Loge, 1874
Oil on canvas, 80 x 64 cm
Courtauld Institute Gallery, London

16. Pierre-Auguste Renoir
Bal au Moulin de la Galette, 1876
Oil on canvas, 131 x 175 cm
Musée d'Orsay, Paris

17. Édouard Manet
Plum Brandy, 1877-78
Oil on canvas, 73.6 x 50.2 cm
National Gallery of Art, Washington

18. Edgar Degas
Absinthe (The Absinth Drinker), 1875-76
Oil on canvas, 92 x 68 cm
Musée d'Orsay, Paris

19. Édouard Manet
Portrait of Stéphane Mallarmé, 1876
Oil on canvas, 27 x 36 cm
Musée d'Orsay, Paris

20. Édouard Manet
Autumn. Portrait of Mery Laurent, 1881
Oil on canvas, 73 x 51 cm
Musée des Beaux-Arts, Nancy

21. Pierre-Auguste Renoir
Jeanne Samary in a Low-Necked Dress (La Rêverie), 1877
Oil on canvas, 56cm x 47cm
Pushkin Museum, Moscow

22. Vincent van Gogh
L'Arlesienne (Madame Ginoux), 1890
Oil on canvas, 60 x 50 cm
National Gallery of Modern Art, Rome

23. Mary Cassatt
Lady at the Tea Table, 1883-85
Oil on canvas, 73.7 x 61 cm
The Metropolitan Museum of Art, New York, Gift of Mary Cassatt, 1923

24. Vincent van Gogh
La Berceuse (Madame Roulin Rocking the Cradle), 1889
Oil on canvas, 92 x 73 cm
Kröller-Müller Museum, Otterlo

25. Paul Cézanne
La Dame au livre, 1902-04
Oil on canvas, 66 x 50.1 cm
Phillips Collection, Whashington

26. Paul Cézanne
Woman in Blue, circa 1904
Oil on canvas, 88.5 x 72 cm
The State Hermitage Museum, St. Petersburg

27. Camille Pissarro
Self-portrait, 1873
Oil on canvas, 56 x 46.7 cm
Musée d'Orsay, Paris

28. Paul Cézanne
Self-portrait with Beret, circa 1875
Oil on canvas, 53 x 38cm
The State Hermitage Museum, St. Petersburg

29. Claude Monet
Impression, soleil levant (Impression, Sunrise), 1872
Oil on canvas, 48 x 63 cm
Musée Marmottan, Paris

30. Claude Monet
La Gare Saint-Lazare (Saint-Lazare Station), 1877
Oil on canvas, 75.5 x 104 cm
Musée d'Orsay, Paris

31. Claude Monet
Cliffs at Etretat, 1886
Oil on canvas, 65 x 81 cm
Pushkin Museum, Moscow

32. Claude Monet
Houses of Parliament, London, Sun Breaking Through the Fog, 1904
Oil on canvas, 81 x 92 cm
Musée d'Orsay, Paris

33. Alfred Sisley
Regatta at Molesey, 1874
Oil on canvas, 66 x 91.5 cm
Musée d'Orsay, Paris

34. Claude Monet
Rue Saint-Denis, Paris. Festivities of 30 June 1878, 1878
Oil on canvas, 81 x 50.5 cm
Musée des Beaux-Arts, Rouen

35. Édouard Manet
Boating, 1874
Oil on canvas, 97.2 x 130.2 cm
The Metropolitan Museum of Art, New York, H.O. Havemeyer Collection, Bequest of Mrs. H.O. Havemeyer

36. Édouard Manet
Chez le Père Lathuille, 1879
Oil on canvas, 93 x 112 cm
Musée des Beaux-Arts, Tournai

37. Édouard Manet
Woman with fans, 1873-74
Oil on canvas, 113 x 166 cm
Musée d'Orsay, Paris

38. Édouard Manet
Nana, 1877
Oil on canvas, 150 x 116 cm
Kunsthalle, Hamburg

39. Berthe Morisot
The Cradle, 1872
Oil on canvas, 56 x 46 cm
Musée d'Orsay, Paris

40. Pierre-Auguste Renoir
Madame Georges Charpentier and her Children, 1878
Oil on canvas, 153.7 x 190.2 cm
The Metropolitan Museum of Art, New York, Catharine Lorillard Wolfe Collection, Wolfe Fund, 1907

41. Edgar Degas
Miss La La at the Cirque Fernando, 1879
Oil on canvas, 117 x 77.5 cm
National Gallery, London

42. Edgar Degas
Dancer at the Photographer's, circa 1875
Oil on canvas, 65 x 50 cm
Pushkin Museum, Moscow

43. Edgar Degas
At Ballet, 1874-76
Oil on canvas, 69 x 49 cm
Städelsches Kunstinstitut und Städtische Galerie, Frankfurt

44. Edgar Degas
The Orchestra of the Opera, circa 1868
Oil on canvas, 56.5 x 46 cm
Musée d'Orsay, Paris

45. Camille Pissarro
Boulevard Montmartre in Paris. Sunny Afternoon, 1897
Oil on canvas, 74 x 92.8 cm
The State Hermitage Museum, St. Petersburg

46. Camille Pissarro
Boïeldieu Bridge, Rouen, 1896
Oil on canvas, 54 x 65 cm
Musée d'Orsay, Paris

47. Claude Monet
Stacks of Wheat (End of Day, Autumn), 1890-91
Oil on canvas, 65.8 x 101 cm
The Art Institute, Chicago, Mr. and Mrs. Lewis Larned Coburn Memorial Collection

48. Claude Monet
Stacks of Wheat (Late Summer), 1891
Oil on canvas, 60.5 x 100.5 cm
Musée d'Orsay, Paris

49. Claude Monet
Rouen Cathedral, Morning Sun, 1894
Oil on canvas, 106 x 73 cm
Musée d'Orsay, Paris

50. Claude Monet
Rouen Cathedral, Midday, 1894
Oil on canvas, 100 x 65 cm
Pushkin Museum, Moscow

	Timeline of Impressionism	Historical events
1859	Manet rejected at the Salon. Degas in Italy.	Piedmont defeats Austria in the Second War of Italian Independence; gains Lombardy.
1860	Berthe Morisot meets Manet and becomes his pupil. Baudelaire rejected by the Académie Française.	Italy: Garibaldi's March.
1862	Cézanne leaves his bank job to paint. Monet at Le Havre. In Florence the artists of the Caffé Michelangelo exhibit landscapes: the paintings are described as "macchie" – patches.	Abolition of slavery in the United States. Victor Hugo publishes *Les misérables*.
1863	Salon des Refusés: paintings exhibited by Manet (*Le Déjeuner sur l'Herbe*), Pissarro, Guillaumin, Cézanne; Monet working at Fontainebleau.	Battle of Gettysburg in the American Civil War.
1865	Manet exhibits his *Olympia* at the Salon, provoking lively controversy.	Lincoln assassinated. Death of Proudhon; his *Principe d'Art* is published posthumously. *Alice in Wonderland* by Lewis Carroll. Florence capital of Italy.
1870	Franco-Prussian War: Pissarro and Monet flee to England. Bazille is killed in action.	18 July: Franco-Prussian War, Napoleon III defeated at Sedan; Third Republic proclaimed (4 September). The Bersaglieri enter Rome at the Porta Pia.
1871		Paris Commune (March-May).
1873	Van Gogh working in London for over a year. Cézanne settles at Auvers-sur-Oise.	Death of Napoleon III. Nietzsche publishes *The Birth of Tragedy*.
1874	First exhibition of the Impressionists, in the photographer Nadar's studio in Paris.	
1876	Second exhibition of the Impressionists. Renoir: *Bal au Moulin de la Galette*. Mallarmé publishes *Après-midi d'une faune,* illustrated by Manet.	

	Timeline of Impressionism	Historical events
1877	Third exhibition of the Impressionists.	Death of Courbet. Edison invents phonograph.
1879	Fourth exhibition of the Impressionists.	Pasteur discovers rabies vaccine. Edison invents electric light-bulb. Dual Alliance between Germany and Austria-Hungary.
1880	Fifth exhibition of the Impressionists; Gauguin also exhibits.	Rodin commissioned to make the *Gates of Hell*. Dostoyevsky publishes *The Brothers Karamazov*.
1881	Sixth exhibition of the Impressionists; Monet and Renoir do not exhibit. Manet is made a Chevalier de la Légion d'Honneur.	Tsar Alexander II assassinated. Verga: *I Malavoglia*, D'Annunzio: *Canto novo*. French protectorate in Tunisia.
1882	Seventh exhibition of the Impressionists.	Triple Alliance of Germany, Austria-Hungary and Italy.
1883	Death of Manet. Durand-Ruel organizes exhibitions of Impressionist works in London, Berlin and Rotterdam.	Death of Karl Marx and Richard Wagner. First journey of the Orient Express.
1886	Last exhibition of the Impressionists: 17 artists take part. School of Pont-Aven forms around Gauguin.	Zola publishes *L'œuvre*, Fénéon *Les impressionnistes in 1886*, De Amicis *Cuore*.
1890	Monet settles at Giverny. Death of Vincent van Gogh.	
1892	Monet starts work on his *Rouen Cathedral* cycle.	
1895	First exhibition by Cézanne at Vollard's gallery.	Lumière brothers' Cinematograph.
1903	Death of Pissarro and Gauguin. Foundation of the Salon d'Automne.	
1905	Major Impressionist exhibition in London.	Einstein's Theory of Relativity.

Biographies of the main Artists

Camille Pissarro
(Saint-Thomas, 1830 – Paris, 1903)
Born in the West Indies on 10 July 1830, the son of a Portuguese Jewish father and a Creole mother. In 1855 he attended the École des Beaux-Arts in Paris and later the Académie Suisse, where he met Monet. Though his paintings were regularly accepted at the Salon from 1859 to 1869, he made no secret of his dislike of the old-fashioned rules taught in the academies. In 1863 he chose, as a sign of solidarity, to exhibit at the Salon des Refusés, and would often discuss art with Manet, Cézanne and Renoir at the Café Guerbois. During the war of 1870, while the Prussians occupied his home (destroying all the paintings), he was a refugee in London, where he painted landscapes and views of Norwood and the area around Crystal Palace south of the city. He exhibited at Durand-Ruel's London gallery. Returning to France, he lived at Louveciennes and Pontoise, where he was soon joined by Cézanne and together they explored the technique of painting in the open air. In 1874 he took part in the first Impressionist exhibition, and indeed was the only artist to contribute to all of them.
In spite of the simplicity and innocence of his subjects, Pissarro was harshly criticized for his stylistic innovations. In 1884 he moved to Eragny, and the next year, influenced by Seurat, briefly experimented with pointillism. After 1892 he returned to the Impressionist style, to which he remained essentially faithful until his death.

Édouard Manet
(Paris, 1832-1883)
Édouard Manet was born on 23 January 1832. His father was a judge and head of staff at the Ministry of Justice. The young Édouard had a classical education and was intended for a career in the navy, but failed the examinations and persuaded his father to allow him to devote himself to painting. From 1850 to 1856 he studied with the academician Thomas Couture; he frequented the Louvre and travelled in Italy, the Netherlands, Germany and Austria. In 1859 he submitted his *Absinthe Drinker* to the Salon; it was rejected, but in 1861 the jury accepted and praised his *Spanish Guitarist*. On 23 October 1863 he married Suzanne Leenhoff; *Le Déjeuner sur l'Herbe* was rejected at the Salon in that year and he then submitted it to the Salon des Refusés, where it caused a scandal and ferocious arguments, which broke out again with even greater violence over his *Olympia* two years later. These two paintings brought him the enthusiastic admiration of the young artists who used to meet at the Café Guerbois and the Nouvelle Athènes.
In the years that followed he continued to prefer figure paintings, portraits and general scenes, such as his last great work *A Bar at the Folies-Bergère* (1881). He died in Paris on 30 April 1883.

Edgar Degas
(Paris, 1834-1917)
Born in Paris on 19 July 1834 into a wealthy family, the father a rich banker. After high school Edgar briefly attended the studio of the painter Barrias, and then the courses given by Henri Lamothe, a follower of Ingres, at the École des Beaux-Arts. In 1854 he travelled to Naples, returning to Italy in 1856 to stay in Florence with his uncle, the barone Bellelli. He travelled to Rome, Viterbo, Orvieto, Perugia, Assisi and back to Florence, where he began his painting *The Bellelli Family*. From 1860 to 1865, under the influence of Ingres and the great Italian masters, he devoted himself to painting history and myth; but around 1865, partly as a result of meeting Manet and the artists of the Café

Guerbois, he gradually made the contemporary world the subject of his art. In 1872 Degas began to frequent the world of the Opéra. After visiting America (New Orleans), he took part in the first Impressionist exhibition, in 1874, showing ten works. His first sculpture, in wax, dates from 1881. In the following years he remained active despite worsening eyesight; in 1886 he showed a series of ten nudes in pastel at the eighth and last Impressionist group exhibition. He travelled again in Italy, Spain, and Morocco before 1890, but then steadily became more isolated and died in Paris on 27 September 1917.

Paul Cézanne

(Aix-in-Provence, 1839-1906)
Born 19 January 1839, into a well-off middle-class family. In 1852 he entered the Collège Bourbon where he studied the Humanities and made friends with the writer Émile Zola, with whom he kept up a steady correspondence. In 1858 he enrolled to study Law in Aix-in-Provence, but spent much time at the École des Belles Arts; finally in 1861 he overcame his father's objections and was allowed to move to Paris and study painting. He attended the Académie Suisse, where he met Pissarro, Renoir, Monet, Sisley and Bazille. His own achievements were discouraging, and he agreed to work in his father's bank; but before long he was back in Paris: Zola introduced him to the Impressionists and invited him to the meetings at the Café Guerbois where young painters gathered around the charismatic figure of Manet. At the Salon des Refusés in 1863 Cézanne was one of the few who appreciated Manet's revolutionary work. In 1869 he met Hortense Fiquet, a model, who bore him a son but only became his wife in 1886. Rejected on many occasions at the Salon, he exhibited in the first of the Impressionists' shows (1874) and the third (1877). He felt a need, though, to carry on his experimentation in his own way; but the works he produced during his isolation were savaged by the critics and even by his friend Zola: it was the end of their friendship. He was discouraged, and decided to retire to L'Estaque in the south of France. After his father's death in 1877 he alternated between living in Provence and taking trips to Paris and other parts of France, concentrating entirely on his painting in his final years. The art world ignored him until 1895, when the dealer Vollard organized his first "one-man show" in a Paris gallery: it aroused great interest, and Cézanne became officially an important artist. In 1906 he had a heart attack while painting outdoors at Aix, and died few days later at the age of 67.

Alfred Sisley

(Paris, 1839 – Moret-sur-Loing, Paris, 1899)
Born in Paris on 30 October 1839 to English parents; his father, a businessman, tried to get him to study commerce, but with no sucess. In 1862 Sisley attended Charles Gleyre's studio in Paris, where he became a friend of Bazille, Renoir and Monet. Long discussions in the Café Guerbois led him first to an enthusiasm for the art of Corot, Courbet and Daubigny, and then to painting in the open. The war of 1870-71 ruined his father, and from then until his death he lived in poverty. He took part in the first three Impressionist shows and that of 1882. Though much appreciated by the others, he nevertheless remained rather isolated from the group, not least because of his introverted character. He was virtually ignored by the critics and collectors, and never in his lifetime enjoyed the same reputation or financial success as the group's other members. He devoted himself to landscapes, especially at Argenteuil, where he spent long periods staying with Monet, and on boat trips on the Seine between Bougival and Marly-le-Roi. His work draws much inspiration from the

English painting tradition: from Turner, in particular, he derived a clear and luminous palette. His use of broad, well-defined brushstrokes has similarities with Manet and Pissarro. In 1882 he moved to Moret-sur-Loing, where he died on 29 January 1899 of cancer of the throat.

Claude Monet

(Paris, 1840 – Giverny, 1926)

Born in Paris on 14 November 1840, the second son of Claude-Adolphe, a shop-keeper, and Louise-Justine. In 1845 the family moved to Le Havre, where Claude spent his childhood and adolescence, and where he began to draw portraits and caricatures. At an early age he showed a considerable interest in painting; his first teacher was Ochard, a pupil of David's, but he was most influenced by meeting Eugène Boudin, the famous landscape artist, who taught him to paint in the open air.

In 1857 his mother died, and the young Monet was looked after by his aunt. Though his family objected, he went to Paris in 1859, where he met Cézanne and Pissarro. In 1861 he left for Algeria on his military service, but this was interrupted by illness in 1862. Returning to Paris he met Renoir, Bazille and Sisley: this was the start of the Impressionists as a group. In 1865 he exhibited for the first time at the Salon. His work met with patchy success. When the Franco-Prussian War broke out in 1870, he left for England, where he discovered Turner, a fundamental influence in his artistic growth to full maturity. After living at Argenteuil he settled at Giverny in 1883, and never moved again, though he visited many European countries including Italy: Venice, in particular, the subject of his famous *Views*. During the First World War he painted his *Waterlilies*, which he gave to the French nation on the day of victory. His sight began to fail from 1908 onwards, and in the end he became almost blind, but continued to paint. He died at Giverny on 26 December 1926.

Frederic Bazille

(Montpellier, 1841 – Beaune-la-Rolande, 1870)

Born in 1841 in Montpellier, into a Protestant middle-class family from the south of France. Moved to Paris in 1862 to study Medicine, but turned to painting after meeting Monet, Sisley and Renoir in the studio of the artist Charles Gleyre. In long discussions with friends at the Café Guerbois he came to admire the outdoor "impressions" of Eugène Boudin and Sisley. The latter became a close friend, and they used to go together paint the woods of Fontainebleau, Honfleur and other places dear to the Impressionists. His style matured during his annual holidays at the family villa at Meric on the banks of the Lez; in 1870 he left his workshop in the rue Visconti and moved to Les Batignolles, where he painted *The artist's studio*. He quickly became one of the group's best known members, both for his talent and for his proverbial kindness. In 1870 he enlisted on the outbreak of the Franco-Prussian War, and was killed the same year in the battle of Beaune-la-Rolande at just 29 years old.

Berthe Morisot

(Bourges, 1841 – Paris, 1895)

Born on 14 January 1841, the daughter of a high-ranking civil servant working for the Auditor's Office, who taught her to draw and passed on to her his passion for painting. She showed early talent, but as a woman could not enter the École des Beaux-Arts, and so studied privately in the studio of the academician Joseph Guichard. He introduced her to Corot, who encouraged her to paint in the open air. In 1864 her work was accepted at the Salon, and she exhibited there regularly until 1873. On 12 December 1874 she married Édouard Manet's brother Eugène, and bore him a daughter, Julie, in 1878. That year she also took part in the Impressionists' first exhibition, and contributed to all their subsequent shows except that of 1879, when her mother's duties prevented her. With her husband, Berthe funded the last of these shows (1886) and took an active part in selecting the artists. She later exhibited with success in the galleries of Petit and Durand-Ruel, both in France and in the United States. Renoir was a frequent visitor in her household in the winter of 1885-86; he became one of her best friends, and was indeed influenced by her painting style. In her last years Berthe continued to paint and exhibit works of great beauty, until her death at the age of 54.

Pierre-Auguste Renoir
(Limoges, 1841 – Cagnes-sur-Mer, 1919)
Sixth of the seven children of Leonard, a tailor, and Marguerite Merlet, a factory worker. In 1844 the family moved to Paris, and the young Renoir worked as an apprentice porcelain painter. On entering the École des Beaux-Arts he studied under Émile Signol and Charles Gleyre, whose studio he frequented, meeting Bazille, Monet and Sisley and forming the "Group des Batignolles" – the future Impressionists. In 1874 he took part in the first Impressionist exhibition. In 1881 and 1882 he visited Algeria and Italy, and was much struck by the Renaissance painting there, which led him by degrees away from the Impressionist style.
He continued to frequent Berthe Morisot's home, where he met other painters as well as critics, poets and authors. On 14 April 1890 he married Aline Charigot in Paris town hall. In May and June that year he exhibited at the Salon for the last time. From 1899 on he lived at Cagnes-sur-Mer, between Nice and Antibes. In May 1900 he showed ten canvasses at the Paris Exposition Universelle; on 16 August he was made a Chevalier de la Légion d'Honneur. He died on 2 December 1919.

Gustave Caillebotte
(Paris, 1848 – Gennevilliers, Paris, 1894)
Born into a rich industrial textiles family; studied Law and graduated in 1870. In 1872 he attended Léon Bonnat's workshop to prepare for the entrance competition at the École des Beaux-Arts, which he passed brilliantly the following year. On his father's death in 1874 he inherited a considerable estate, which made it possible for him to devote himself to painting. He met Degas, who introduced him to the other Impressionists; and at the invitation of Renoir and Rouart took part in their second exhibition in 1876 at the gallery of Paul Durand-Ruel; he also began to buy Impressionist works. He provided funding and organization for the shows of 1879, 1880 and 1882, and for the transfer to New York with Durand-Ruel in 1885. In 1888 he took part in the Brussels "Salon des XX" which to some extent accepted neo-Impressionist trends.
He died at 46 years old after a short illness on 21 February 1894. In his Will he left sixty-five paintings to the State, on condition they were put on show at the Musée du Luxembourg in Paris, the museum of modern art of the time (they are now in the Musée d'Orsay). His executors (his brother Martial and Renoir) faced opposition from the official artists of the Academy, who only accepted thirty-eight of these in the end.

Vincent van Gogh
(Groot Zundert, 1853 – Auvers-sur-Oise, 1890)
Eldest son of a Protestant pastor; after completing school he worked for a firm of art dealers first at The Hague and then, from 1873, in London. In 1875 he was moved to the Paris office, but was sacked the following year and returned to the Netherlands. After trying one thing and another, he moved to Mons in 1878, where he preached to the miners; but he took their side during strikes, and was sacked by the local religious authorities. He began to draw, and after deciding to devote himself to painting left for Brussels. He next moved to Nuenen, where he painted masterpieces such as the *The*

Potato Eaters in 1885; his father died the same year. In 1886 he joined his brother Theo in Paris, where he discovered Impressionist painting and Japanese art, and met Toulouse-Lautrec and Guillaumin. In 1888 he left for Arles, where he painted *Flowering Orchard*, *Cafe Terrace at Night*, *The Bedroom,* and other pictures. He shared the "Yellow House" with Gauguin, but after a period of happy mutual stimulation, the two artists quarrelled and Gauguin left again: seized with despair, van Gogh cut off an ear-lobe; he was taken into care and transferred to the Saint-Rémy asylum, where he painted works including *Cypresses* and *Starry Night*. He then left for Auvers-sur-Oise, encouraged and supported by his brother and Dr. Gachet. In 1890 he painted *Cornfield with Crows*. On 27 July that year he shot himself with a pistol, and died two days later.

Henri de Toulouse-Lautrec
(Albi, 1864 – Malromé, Bordeaux, 1901)
Born 24 November 1864, into a very old noble family. Began drawing as a child, during long spells of inactivity forced on him by poor health, aggravated by two falls which had broken both femurs and stopped his legs developing properly.
In 1872 the family moved to Paris, where his father introduced him to the painter Princeteau, who encouraged him in painting subjects on horseback. In 1882 he went to learn in Bonnat's studio, and the following year benefited greatly from lessons with Ferdinand Cormon. He met the Impressionists and studied their works, in particular those of Degas and van Gogh, though he never exhibited in their shows. He became a habitué of Montmartre, the ballet, theatres and *café-concerts* which became the backdrop to his most famous paintings. He worked with many newspaper and reviews as a cartoonist, experimenting with new engraving techniques and designing some thirty posters which caused a great stir with their stylistic novelty, derived in part from his interest in Japanese prints. He made a series of about forty paintings devoted to Paris brothels; and the ensuing scandal helped to build his legend as a wicked artist and outlaw.
He died on 9 September 1901, at the age of just 37.

Selected Bibliography

J. Rewald, *The history of Impressionism*, London 1980 (4th revised edition)
R. Shiff, *Cézanne and the end of Impressionism: a study of the theory, technique and critical evaluation of modern art*, Chicago 1984
J. Redwall, *Studies in Impressionism*, London 1985
T. Denis, *The age of the Impressionists*, London 1992
G.P. Weisberg, *Beyond Impressionism: the naturalist impulse in European art 1860-1905*, London 1992
B. Denvir, *The chronicle of Impressionism: an intimate diary of the lives an world of the great artists*, London 1993
S. Adams, *The Barbizon school and the origins of Impressionism*, London 1994
J. Medina, *Cézanne and modernism: the poetics of painting*, Albany 1995
N. Mowll Mathews (ed.), *Cassatt: a retrospective*, New York 1996
A. Callen, *The art of Impressionism: painting technique and the making of modernity*, New Haven-London 2000
A. Cunningham, *Essential Impressionists*, Bath 2000
P.H. Tucker, *The Impressionists at Argenteuil*, Washington 2000
D. Wildenstein, *Monet, or The triumph of Impressionism*, Köln-London 2003
J. House, *Impressionism: paint and politics*, New Haven-London 2004
S. Lemoine (ed.), *Paintings in the Musée d'Orsay*, London 2004
R.R. Brettel, *Gauguin and Impressionism*, New Haven-London 2005
S.M. Søndergaad, *Women in Impressionism: from mythical feminine to modern woman*, Milan 2003
P. Assouline, *Discovering Impressionism: the life of Paul Durand-Ruel*, New York-London 2005
A. Dumas (ed.), *Inspiring Impressionism: the Impressionists and the art of the past*, Denver-London 2007
J. House, *Impressionists by the sea*, London 2007
M. Tompkins Lewis (ed.), *Critical readings in Impressionism and Post-Impressionism: an anthology*, Berkeley-London 2007
J.H. Rubin, *Impressionism and the modern landscape: productivity, technology and urbanization from Manet to van Gogh*, Berkeley-London 2008